AMAZING THINGS

WILL

HAPPEN

AMAZING THINGS WILL HAPPEN

A REAL-WORLD GUIDE ON ACHIEVING SUCCESS AND HAPPINESS

C.C. CHAPMAN

WILEY

John Wiley & Sons, Inc.

Cover image: Tree © Classix/iStockphoto
Cover design: C. Wallace

Published by John Wiley & Sons, Inc., Hoboken, New Jersey.
Published simultaneously in Canada.

For general information about our other products and services, please contact our Customer Care Department within the United States at (800) 762-2974, outside the United States at (317) 572-3993 or fax (317) 572-4002.

Wiley publishes in a variety of print and electronic formats and by print-on-demand. Some material included with standard print versions of this book may not be included in e-books or in print-on-demand. If this book refers to media such as a CD or DVD that is not included in the version you purchased, you may download this material at http://booksupport.wiley.com. For more information about Wiley products, visit www.wiley.com.

Library of Congress Cataloging-in-Publication Data:

Chapman, C. C., 1973-
    Amazing things will happen : a real-world guide on achieving success and happiness / C.C. Chapman.
        p. cm.
    ISBN 978-1-118-34138-4 (cloth); ISBN 978-1-118-42010-2 (ebk);
    ISBN 978-1-118-41662-4 (ebk); ISBN 978-1-118-43411-6 (ebk)
        1. Success. 2. Self-realization. 3. Happiness. 4. Conduct of life. I. Title.
BJ1611.2.C475 2013
650.1—dc23

                                                                        2012036998

Printed in the United States of America

10 9 8 7 6 5 4 3 2 1

For Dylan and Emily,
I hope these words prove to be a valuable travel
companion as you find your own roads less traveled.

Contents

Acknowledgments

Being an author is a beautiful way to make a living, but it is not something that you can ever be successful at on your own. There are always people along the road who help you, and I want to make sure I thank them all.

To every fan, follower, homefry, manager, mentor, and friend, I say thank you. I could never list you all individually, but know that I am grateful for every one of you who has crossed my path over the years.

To my team at John Wiley & Sons, Inc. who saw this book as more than a simple idea and supported me from day one. Shannon, your blunt honesty and challenging thoughts made the book better than I first imagined.

Ann, I missed having you as my copilot on this journey and I look forward to our next adventure together.

To my acorns and squirrels who are always there when I need a nudge of encouragement and a laugh to push through the hard times.

Jane, Clarence, Steve, and JC, you all push and support me at every turn. Whenever I question the direction I'm moving in, a quick chat with any of you confirms if I'm going the right way or not.

Dad and Mom, although you may not fully understand what I do on a daily basis, I know that you love and support me no matter what. You helped me grow into the man I've become, and I can never thank you enough.

Dylan and Emily, you two are how I judge if I'm doing the right things in life. Watching you mature into the young adults that you've become reminds me that I'll leave the world a better place than I found it.

Laura, you are my best friend, and I couldn't live the life I do without you in it. I'm so glad you started that tape fight so many years ago and that we've tickled and teased each other ever since. Now and always.

You Choose the Path to Follow

Welcome to *Amazing Things Will Happen*.

The following pages are filled with advice, thoughts, and experiences that you need to take to heart if you want to live a happier and more fulfilling life. They are a collection of lessons I've learned from my experiences and that have been given to me from a variety of people I've met throughout my life. They've served me well and will assist you to move forward in your life.

The smartest people are lifelong students—always learning from those around them and never believing that they know enough. Although our education system may believe that we can learn only from books and in classrooms, the truth is that everything around us is a classroom. To be a better person, you should never stop experiencing and learning new things.

How you get from where you are now to where the amazing things begin to happen is up to you. This is a guide to get you jump-started, push you forward, and motivate you to find your own path.

Preface

You need to know up front what this book is and, more important, what it is not.

People say that the way I live my life inspires them. I had always just sort of shrugged this off with a giggle or a gracious nod and moved on to other things. But as more people told me this, I became inspired to share my approach with the world in the hopes that it helps change others' lives as well.

For years, my podcast *Managing the Gray* has been an outlet to share my diverse knowledge about everything from online marketing to advice on how to have a more successful career. The more listeners commented and reacted to what was said, the clearer it became that focusing on self-improvement, achieving your goals, and living a happier life was what they were most interested in. This book grew out of that show.

This book takes the knowledge I've accumulated over the years and shares it with you. It isn't a life guide, a coaching playbook, or a be-happy-quick manual. It is my personal approach and thoughts on life straight from the heart.

Although many people get lucky, most people who have found a successful balance of life and work have done so through lots of hard work. Life rarely will hand you something without requiring you to put in the time to earn it. You have to do the work!

The words of encouragement and inspirations shared are meant to push you in the direction of which you've always dreamed. Perhaps you will decide to pursue your dreams, change career, make a difference in the world, or follow your passions wherever they lead. A large part of success also calls for taking risks that don't always pay off. You don't get to walk on the path of amazing if you are too scared to risk a bit.

I don't promise the world, but I do promise that if you work hard, stay true to yourself, be a good person, help others, and listen to those around you, amazing things *will* happen.

Short On Time, But Still Crave Amazing Things?

The reality of reading is that most don't make enough time for it.

For those of you who are short on time but still want to learn from this book, I've made it easy for you. Sure, it is cheating a bit, but I'd rather you think of this condensed overview as a little lifehack instead. Hopefully when you have time, you'll come back and read the full thing.

The ideas for this book began forming as my children grew older and began asking lots of questions about their future. Combine that with

1

the constant stream of questions from others asking how to live a happy and fulfilling life and I knew I had to get this book out into the world.

Many people want more money, a new job, or a happier relationship, but they are not willing to put in the time and work to make any of it happen. Those people drive me nuts. There are so many get-rich-quick schemes out there that I wanted to create a road map that people could actually use to achieve their dreams successfully.

Amazing things happen only if you work hard—really hard. And they happen only if you are good to others. No one can do it alone, and it is the people around you who are going to help make your success happen. When you are kind toward others, they will return the kindness to you. Listening and kindness are two skills that don't get taught in school, yet they are crucial for you to succeed in any capacity.

Life is short. You never know if you'll be given tomorrow, so get out there and make the most of it. At its heart, that is what this book is about.

If all these pages were summed up into a single paragraph, they would say:

Amazing Things Will Happen makes it clear that once you figure out what you want out of life, if you work very hard, day in and day out, you can make it happen. But you have to be a good human in addition to doing the work. As you achieve success, never forget to be kind to others. Help those who need it and share everything you've learned with all who ask. Follow these principles in your life, and amazing things will happen.

Still not condensed or short enough for your busy life? I can condense it even further:

Amazing Things Will Happen is a guide to living a good life.

Why a Guide?

Life doesn't come with an instruction manual. Humans are too much of a mixed bag for it to be that easy.

Each of us must find the stories, books, inspirations, and people who inspire us. Those who give you a kick in the right direction or guidance on big decisions.

As such, I'm sharing the words of wisdom that have been shared with me over the years from various intelligent individuals, as well as some words of wisdom I've discovered on my own. Hopefully, these words will speak to you and in turn inspire you as they have me.

If it were as simple as $X + Y = A$ Happy Life, then the world would be a much happier place. And although these words are meant to help each of you, this book can only guide you forward; it cannot give you specific directions.

The path for each of us is unique, and it's up to you to find the way.

How you use this book is up to you.

I've divided the book into rough sections, with the hopes that you can pick and choose what is most impactful to you. The sections are as follows:

1. *Telling the Tale*

    This is where we are right now. Every house needs to be built upon a solid foundation. Once we've established a few essential things, the real fun begins and we can take steps toward making your life more enjoyable.

2. *Taking Stock*

    If you are going to make changes, you first need to identify where you are now and where you want to be. Many people are able to recognize that they must make changes, but they are not sure what to do next. Looking over the edge of a cliff into the unknown below never comes without fear. Some choose to enjoy the view and never take the plunge. But the wise will minimize any dangers they might encounter before jumping in with anticipation.

Taking risks can be immensely rewarding, as long as you are informed of and prepared for the outcomes. And this section is going to ensure that you are.

3. *Time for Change*

Once you've prepared for the big change, it is time to do it. Often, this is when the most obstacles and challenges will arise. It is easy to question if you've made the right decision, but the tips in this section will give you plenty to think about to keep pushing forward.

No one enjoys change, but it is a crucial part of finding and doing what you love in life, so it's important to face it and push through your fears.

4. *Taking the Road Less Traveled*

There isn't a single path that everyone can use to reach the goals they seek. We each make our own success, and that can come only after a lot of trial and error. But the sooner you realize that the journey is part of the enjoyment, the more fun your adventure will be.

There have been plenty of books written about making the decision to do what you love, but not enough has been written about *fully* enjoying the time once you get there. Be sure to come back to this section for inspiration if you get stuck along the way.

Are you ready? Let's go!

Introduction

My Journey So Far

I was born on December 19, at Dartmouth-Hitchcock hospital in Hanover, New Hampshire. My parents had recently graduated from high school and would marry shortly after. They were not financially or emotionally ready to have a child, but through sacrifice and the help of their families, they made it work.

We moved around a lot when I was little, eventually settling in Upper Valley, New Hampshire, which is small-town America at its finest.

It is a slice of America where everyone knows everyone and where some of your high school teachers taught your parents. Every day your path crosses with people to whom you give a knowing nod as you go about your day.

Growing up, I always had tons of energy, and wearing a T-shirt that read, "Look out, here comes trouble," was standard uniform. After my two sisters were born, they gave me new outlets in which to use my energy. I got grounded a lot for doing stupid little things to torment them.

My mother ran a day-care business out of our house. My dad worked numerous jobs, including doing tree work (which he went to college for), working at the post office, delivering potato chips, and for a while, running his own landscaping business. The importance of a strong work ethic was instilled in me at a young age.

I was also fortunate to grow up with both sets of my grandparents close by. We'd see them quite often, and although I loved them all, I was always closest with my dad's father. He loved to fly airplanes, draw, and even had a photography darkroom in his basement.

Grampa Chapman showed me the importance of using my imagination and was the first to expose me to photography. We used to write letters to each other that contained more doodles than words, and we'd make up stories together all the time. He passed away from pancreatic cancer when I was nine, and there's not a day that goes by that I don't miss him. I wish he were here to see that I still use what he taught me to this day.

In fifth grade, my teacher, Susan Pet, encouraged me to join the drama club and cast me as the lead in my first play. I was playing the part of the Lorax from the famous Dr. Seuss book. I instantly fell in love with the stage and the rush of energy you feel from an entertained audience. I have continued to take the stage in various forms throughout my life, and I credit Mrs. Pet for directing me down that path.

Just before I started high school, my family and I moved to West Lebanon, New Hampshire. This was a difficult time to make a transition in a teenager's life, but I tried to make it work.

At my new school, I wasn't popular or an out-cast, although I never really did make a ton of close friends. Participating in band and drama put me in with one crowd, but I also hung out with people from a bunch of other cliques. This taught me that it was more important to be happy with myself than it was to impress other people. This attitude has always served me well, and I utilize it to this day.

At the end of my sophomore year of high school, I began hanging out with a girl named Laura, whom I had met through marching band. We became friends and discovered that we had classes together. The next thing I knew, I was over at her house helping her with homework.

I was a typical teenage boy and was nervous at the emotions I felt for her. One day, however, I decided to take a huge risk by passing her a note that told her how much I liked her. I was scared. She was this beautiful senior girl: the type that you look at and think, "Wouldn't it be amazing if . . . ," but deep down you know it is never going to happen. And here I was telling her I liked her. This could only go badly, right?

In the end, my chance paid off! For months she had been trying to let me know that she liked me, but I didn't realize it. But because I took a risk instead of only hoping and dreaming, I was able to achieve my goal.

Never forget that the worst anyone can ever say is no. But, you'll never hear yes if you don't ask. We began dating immediately and are still together to this day.

Around the same time that we started dating, I experienced another life-changing event: discovering the Internet. I had first fallen in love with computers in fourth grade, when my teacher, Mr. Davenport, first showed me one. But it wasn't until I had secured access to a network account at Dartmouth College that a whole new world opened up to me.

It was 1989—the days where the World Wide Web was mostly text, chat rooms, and e-mail. I'd spend hours every day in a chat room called XYZ. My friends and I would sneak into the computer center on campus to get access to the Macintoshes they had there so that we could play Netrek (the first networked game I'd ever played).

For the first time in my life, I found myself with virtual friends—individuals whom I only knew through the computer screen. We'd talk about our lives, set up times to meet face to face, and get to know one another only through the words we typed on our screens. This opened up a world of possibilities.

High school was ending, and although I was looking at colleges, I wasn't sure where I wanted to go.

After a visit to Bentley University in Waltham, Massachusetts, I fell in love with the school. My guidance counselor told me point blank that I'd never get into the school and that I should look for other options. Being told I couldn't do something didn't sit well with me, so I applied early decision. The day I got my acceptance letter, I proudly marched a copy into the guidance counselor's office and walked out.

As one of the premier business schools in the country, Bentley was an expensive school. I had to work multiple jobs to make it work, but I knew I wanted my degree and I was prepared to do anything to make it a reality.

While at college, I decided to major in computer information systems since I grew up loving computers. In my junior year, I started an e-mail newsletter called "Thoughts" that I sent out to friends; I'd jokingly sign them from "The

Thoughts Master." It included a variety of funny quotes, random musings, inside jokes, and anything else that was on the top of my mind.

These were fun for me to write up and send. When people reacted positively to them, it inspired me to continue creating them. If it made other people happy, it was worth it to find the time to continue writing them.

I also became an active member of Alpha Psi Omega (AΨΩ), the national coed dramatic fraternity.

One of the students who also pledged was Dan Gorgone, a rabid Red Sox fan and movie junkie. We quickly became the best of friends and started a popular campus radio show called "C.C. & The Man" on WBTY. Dan was friends with a budding film student at Emerson College, named Jason Santo, who always needed actors for his class assignments, and he would call on Dan and his acting buddies to serve as cast and crew for his short films.

It wasn't long before Dan and I decided we would try making movies ourselves. On April 2, 1996, after completing our weekly radio show, we decided to make our first short, and Random Foo Pictures was born.

In the last week before I graduated from Bentley, we filmed four different short films. We dreamt of becoming a full-blown production company and making our livings producing films.

Now that graduation was upon me, I knew I needed to find a job and settle down. While Laura and I both loved growing up in small-town America, she wanted a change. There were tons of job opportunities in the Boston area for me, but we decided to look outside of the area and move to wherever I landed a job. Since she worked in health care, she figured she could land on her feet anywhere.

I accepted a job with James Martin & Company doing consulting in their government division. We packed up a moving truck and rented an apartment in the Virginia suburbs, right outside of Washington, DC.

After some initial training, I headed into several months of time known as being "on the beach," which was cutesy consulting speak for not having billable hours.

I decided to use this time to teach myself HTML. The local bookstore had a copy of *HTML For Dummies* and I was on my way.

I spent the next three months teaching myself the programming language. It wasn't easy, but I wanted to make sure I understood it because I knew the Internet was going to be a big part of my future.

When there were no work projects that I could help with, I would teach myself HTML during the day and then work on creating a website for Random Foo Pictures at night.

The site launched in the summer of 1996, and soon we were connecting with other people who had similar dreams of making movies. The world suddenly got smaller, as our little short films could be viewed and enjoyed by others. We'd post photos and movie plots, and others did the same. There were no easy ways to put videos online at the time, so we would trade VHS tapes of our movies through the mail.

Communities of filmmakers began to spring up, and REwind soon became the most-visited one. They served as the go-to location to find out what others were doing, and we used the discussion forums to get to know one another.

REwind hosted movie awards and festivals, and I traveled to South Dakota for one event after one of our films, *Inquisition*, was nominated. It was so exciting to meet the people whom I had known only online. We ended up winning Best Short Film and Best Director. It was the first time I had been given such high praise for something I had created.

Although filmmaking would not become my full time job, I now knew that I had the gift of storytelling. Whatever I did in the future, I knew this would be part of it.

In 1999, our son was born and we moved back to New England to be closer to our families.

It was the height of the dot-com era, and I knew I could find a job easily.

I headed up to Massachusetts to look for a place to live and went on several job interviews. I found a little top floor apartment in Watertown over an Italian grandmother who spoke little English but would leave bags of produce from her garden outside of our door.

I soon accepted a job offer from a telecom company that was the last of my top three choices because the other two didn't offer me a job fast enough.

At my new job, I was responsible for building the company's intranet and eventually was put in charge of a small Web team.

In 2001 I was looking to hire a junior Web developer. It was the height of the dot-com frenzy, so there were many cocky programmers who thought that they could demand anything and get it.

I had been interviewing candidates for a couple of weeks when Tony came in. He had taken several courses in Web development but had no real-world experience yet. Sensing my apprehension, he said, "Listen, I know I haven't worked in this field yet, but I want to learn and will do everything I can to learn how to do anything you ask me to do." His motivation won me over; I had found my programmer.

I got a lot of pushback about hiring Tony, but my argument was that he was working for me. If he didn't work out, I'd fire him, but he had the passion and drive to learn. Tony worked out great and worked every day as hard as I hoped he would.

In addition to Tony, I had a more senior programmer working for me named Donna. She was a great programmer and team member.

When Donna approached me about working remotely one day a week, I saw no reason not to allow it. Telecommuting was brand new, but our company did have the technology set up that made it easy for her to do her job from any computer connected to the Internet. She was a stellar employee who always overdelivered, so I approved her request on the condition that if her performance began to slip, we'd have to stop it.

One day while she was working from home, my manager asked where she was. When I explained, he scolded me for making such a poor management decision, and I was forced to revoke the privilege.

This taught me that not everyone would agree with the decisions I made in my life and career, but if I believed in what I was doing, I had to stick to my guns.

I wasn't ready for the perfect storm that was about to hit my career. Between our company being acquired by a larger one and the dot-com bubble bursting, I found myself laying off my team and, quickly thereafter, being laid off myself.

After I was laid off, I remember sitting at home, thinking about my next move. I now had a baby daughter in addition to my son and a loving wife who, thankfully, had a job. But what was *I* going to do?

Fortunately, I had received a small severance package that allowed me to take the time to find the right opportunity, rather than having to jump at the first thing that looked viable.

I ended up finding employment at Babson College working in the information technology (IT) department, focusing mainly on their intranet.

I was surrounded by people who were doing great work. I worked with individuals from all around the campus, from all offices. It was part of my job to meet with vendors and help choose applications we'd roll out campus wide. It gave me experience working with people at all levels whose experience levels covered the spectrum.

Then, in 2002, back on the personal front, our landlord informed us that he would be selling the house we were living in. We decided now was the perfect time to buy a house for our little family.

Not long after we moved into our new house, I made another big step in my life. On July 2, 2002, I wrote my first blog post. I had always kept a journal, but now I could share my thoughts with the world. I didn't know if anyone was going to be interested in reading them, but I began blogging regularly.

After blogging for several months and opening up my world to new online communities and making new friends, I would experience another major shift when in December 2004, I got my first iPod.

Although just another portable music device for many, for me it was more. I had discovered a new word: *podcasting*.

I found a community of people at Podcast Alley who were creating a variety of podcasts. I listened to a couple and realized I had everything I needed to try one out. On December 21, 2004, I hit record on my microphone and recorded the first episode of *Reality Bitchslap Radio*.

Because music was an important part of my life, I wanted to include an independent music track on every episode. I had met several artists through my moviemaking endeavors and reached out to them to help with this. They loved the idea of sharing their music on the podcast, and soon we were up and running.

A few other podcasters were doing music-only shows. My college radio days kept crossing my mind, so on January 10, 2005, I recorded the first episode of an all-music podcast called *Accident Hash*.

In those early days of podcasting, it was the Wild West. Many were getting into it, but it was still a small world. When someone new started a show, we'd all go listen and support him or her. Friendships were made, conferences were planned, and companies began to form. It was an exciting time for all of us.

Back at my day job, I was growing stagnant in my position and realized that I wanted to use the other side of my brain more. Although I loved working with technology, the creative side of me was screaming to come out and play more at work. I discovered an opening in the marketing department for the Webmaster and decided to make an appointment with the manager to discuss it.

I knew that there were more opportunities to being a Webmaster than simply maintaining the website, and I was excited to help the school take online technology to the next level. After some discussion, along with a title change to Digital Marketing Manager, they hired me for the role.

While this was happening, I had already established a name for myself in the podcasting world. I was one of the first podcasters signed by a fledgling company and was paid to podcast. I was also the project manager for a site known as the Podsafe Music Network, which empowered artists to upload tracks with a license for podcasters to legally play them. *Accident Hash* had become one of the most popular podcasts in the world, with a legion of fans known as homefries, and I was regularly speaking on music rights and podcasting at industry conferences, including my first international trip to a conference in Germany.

One of the first things I did in my new role at Babson was send myself to an Ad Club of Boston event. It was billed as having "some of the best and brightest" in attendance and on stage. I didn't go to school for marketing—I had learned by using the guerrilla tactics we had adopted with film-making and podcasting. I thought this would be a perfect way to get more knowledge about what experts in the industry were doing.

This single event would once again be one of those decisions in my life that changed so much.

At the conference, I ran into my friend John Wall, whom I had met through his podcast, *The M Show*. We made our way toward each other, and he introduced me to the person with him.

"C.C., this is Joseph Jaffe."

I had been listening to Joe's podcast, *Across the Sound*, for a long time. It was the only podcast that focused on the shift from traditional marketing to the more social and connected world that was developing online. Turns out he was a homefry and a fan of my podcast. We shook hands and had a few drinks, and it was the start of a great friendship and soon-to-be business partnership.

I returned to work full of enthusiasm. I had gone to the conference questioning myself, but I left knowing that I knew more about the coming wave of change than the so-called experts did. We were going to do amazing things.

I still wanted to do more. On May 6, 2006, I published the first episode of a new podcast called *Managing the Gray*. I hoped it would help other people better understand and embrace the new world of online marketing and social media.

The name came about after a conversation with my manager at Babson. She asked how I was dealing with the change from IT to marketing. I told her in the IT world things were very black and white—the program either worked or it didn't, and decisions were much easier. She grinned and told me, "Yeah, in this world there is very little black or white. You need to learn to manage the gray."

So, back at my day job, we had started a new campus-wide initiative to make the school more digital. What started out as the college president wishing to be able to get the latest school team sports scores grew into a plan to update the way the entire college used technology.

Consultants were brought in, meetings were held with various organizations on campus, reams of notes were assembled, and plans were made. We presented the plan with a bare-bones budget to the trustees and waited for approval.

The verdict came back approving only a sliver of what was proposed. All of the hard work and plans to bring the school into the future were crushed.

At that point, I knew it was time to move on. I didn't know what I was going to do, but I knew that I needed to be doing something greater than what I was doing in my current role. I needed to work with forward thinkers who saw the changes happening around us and were not afraid to make them as well. Technology was opening up so many new doors, and I needed to be at the forefront of it.

I decided to send an e-mail to my friends Mitch Joel and Joseph Jaffe to see how they were doing, to tell them that I had decided that night to start looking for a new job, and to ask if they had any advice for me.

It turned out that Joe was forming a new marketing agency, and he asked if I wanted to be part of it. Working for a start-up was a risky move, but it also included a pay raise and I'd be making the sort of difference that I was dreaming about.

I joined Joe's new company, crayon, as a vice president of new marketing. The company was a small nine-person team that Joe had assembled, and we planned to shake up the world.

We were a truly remote company, with all of the employees working out of their homes around the country and one in England. Our office was in the virtual world of Second Life, and one of my first tasks was to work with a developer to design and build our island.

One of the biggest projects I worked on as part of this company was bringing the Coca-Cola Company into Second Life as part of an initiative known as Virtual Thirst. Working with such a well-known brand on a high-profile project was a rush for me. Plus, I was in my element: the project was the perfect mix of creativity and business strategy. To this day, it remains one of my favorite projects I've ever worked on.

Start-ups often hit lots of bumps along the way, and crayon was no different. At that point in time, we were barely making payroll and things were getting tight.

I told myself that if it ever got to the point where I received no paycheck, I would move on. If I was going to be without income, I wanted to be in the position to control my own destiny. Regrettably, that day came, and one of the toughest phone calls I ever had to make was when I told Joe I was leaving the agency to pursue freelancing full time.

While working on the Virtual Thirst project, I had become good friends with the other project manager, Steve Coulson. He was the opposite of me in so many ways, and yet we clicked. Shortly after I left, he did as well for his own reasons.

When word got out that we were both on the market, companies started calling to see if they could hire us as a team.

Although this surprised us, we wondered if it might make sense to do something together instead of on our own or for someone else.

I traveled to New Jersey, where Steve lived, and over breakfast and lots of coffee, we decided to form The Advance Guard.

TAG, as we called it, was going to be a social marketing agency focusing on helping brands create engaging online experiences. The company name was inspired by a quote from Herman Melville: "We are the pioneers of the world; the advance guard, sent on through the wilderness of untried things, to break a new path in the New World that is ours."

We worked on a lot of groundbreaking projects, from bringing American Eagle Outfitters and their sub-brands fully into social media, to setting up a live Web cam of a talking teddy bear that spoke its followers' tweets to showcase the technology of Verizon FiOS, to sending out to influencers glass jars containing artifacts of a personal shark attack for Discovery Channel. We helped clients be strategic, social, and creative in all that they did.

We worked closely with a company called Campfire, and one day over lunch with the team, they surprised us by asking what we thought about being acquired by them. From the beginning, our goal was to do a lifetime of good work, and selling was never something we had wanted or planned for. But, after months of conversations, legal reviews, and everything else that goes into something like this, we signed on the dotted line.

During the following months, I realized something I had known in my heart for a long time. True happiness for me was never going to be achievable as long as I was working for anyone else. There will always be difference of opinions, personalities, and approaches since every human is different.

After my 12 months of required service were up, we came to a mutual parting of the ways. The timing was perfect because I had been working on writing *Content Rules* with Ann Handley, and it was about to hit shelves. It would be great to be able to focus on that.

Once I was on the market again, I had several offers to join other agencies, but I didn't want to jump into anything immediately. I wanted to give solo entrepreneurship a go and see how it went.

That brings us to today and to my decision to write this book. I now make a living speaking, consulting, and creating, and I've never been happier. Every day presents me with a new set of challenges and opportunities, and as a freelancer, if I ever slow my hustle—even for a bit—things could dry up. So I rise every morning ready to attack the day and work hard to make it as successful as possible.

There are days when I miss the fast-paced brainstorming sessions of agency life. I often ponder what it would be like to work directly for a brand in control for the long haul instead of working only on campaigns and projects. But overall, I couldn't be happier with the decisions I've made.

Life is a constant path forking in different directions, and you never know where it might take you. It has been a beautifully strange trip so far. Today I live my life doing what I love.

I live life as a Passion Hit.

1

How to Be a Passion Hit

Passion Hits are people who are able to make a living doing what they love.

You want to do what you love, or you wouldn't be reading this book. You want to find a way to spend every day working on that single thing that fills you with glee thinking about it.

Those who decide to make their passion their work and keep pushing forward no matter what are Passion Hits, a play on the word *passionate*.

My official definition for my made-up word:

Passion Hit—(noun) A person who has discovered his or her true passion in life and found a way to make it his or her livelihood.

Most entrepreneurs are also Passion Hits. If you dedicate that many hours of a day to your business, you've got to be at least a little bit passionate about it. Sure, some do it only for the money or to solve a problem, but the successful ones are also the passionate ones.

They include people such as Jason McCarthy, who after bravely serving our country as a Green Beret wanted to start an American manufacturing company that could live up to military standards as well as the everyday traveler. He focused his energy on starting the GORUCK brand.

Ellen McGirt always had a love for finding, capturing, and sharing the stories of others. She has interviewed chief executive officers, U.S. presidents, celebrities, and regular people across the country. She is currently a senior writer for *Fast Company* magazine.

AJ and Melissa Leon wanted to work and travel together. They formed Misfit Inc. to make both a reality. They now live on the road and help make the world a better place with each new project their team takes on.

Zack Arias is a poster child for the fact that hard, constant work can make dreams come true. He is now one of the best professional photographers in Atlanta and beyond. His style of using only one light when shooting has grown into a series of courses that he sells himself and teaches around the world.

Chris Penn and Chris Brogan were not finding the level of interaction and teaching that they had hoped for at other conferences so they began PodCamp to create a forum for the interaction they wanted. Since that first event in Boston, people have hosted PodCamps around the globe that have educated and networked tens of thousands of people.

Each of these people has a unique story to tell, but every one of them exemplifies the values that a Passion Hit believes in.

I wanted as many people as possible to be inspired by these stories, so I started my Web series Passion Hit TV (http://www.passionhit.tv). I'll be adding new stories there all the time, so be sure to subscribe, and if you have ideas of new Passion Hits that I should interview, you can e-mail me.

The hope and goal is that by the time you finish reading these pages, you'll be inspired enough to set off on your own journey to be a Passion Hit doing what you love. Be sure to let me know how it goes!

2

Trust Your Gut

You can read all the books, attend all the lectures, and listen to all the advice. But living the life you've always dreamed about comes down to one person making the decision to do so—and that person is *you*.

From the smallest decision about which way to turn when you're lost, to the biggest decisions that affect your career and your family, you should always follow one rule that won't lead you astray:

Trust your gut instinct.

You've been there before. You're about to do something, and you get a feeling that perhaps you shouldn't. This isn't that little voice in your head warning of danger, but something much deeper and internal that feels like something is off. Likewise it is the feeling you get inside when an idea is so exciting that you know you have to act on it.

Ever read an e-mail with an offer that feels a bit too good to be true? Met someone at a cocktail party and instantly known that he was someone you need get to know better?

We all wish the feeling was always there, but it isn't. It seems to come and go when it wants. But when it does show up, we must learn to listen to it.

Do you listen to your gut? Think back. Has it ever led you astray?

We all agree to do things we don't want to do. We say no when we want to say yes because we worry about the possible repercussions. Perhaps there is something we've always wanted to do—have been dying to do even—but we don't because we worry about what others might think.

Instead, trust your gut. Learn to embrace that feeling and go in the direction it tells you even if it isn't the direction you were planning on going.

CHAPTER

Take Stock

There will come a time when you'll feel the yearning to make a change in your life. Maybe you realize you aren't as happy as you could be. Perhaps you want to do more with your life than what you are currently doing.

Mine came one day while I was commuting to work. It hit me that I wasn't passionate about my job anymore.

You may feel like, whatever it is that you are doing in life, you want to do better. You may feel this way about your relationships, your career, or another aspect of your life that you realize isn't where you would like it to be.

Many ignore these feelings and instead bury them in a deep, dark corner of their brain. Sometimes you have to do this. It is not always a great time to make a major life shift, and you should never blindly jump over the edge without careful thinking.

Before making any changes, you need to be sure that all of your bases are covered. Look at it from all angles. Do a solid review of your bills, income, and commitments so that you have a clear picture of everything in your life that may be affected. Play the Devil's advocate and think about the worst things that could possibly happen if you were to make a change.

Nothing bad ever comes of being careful before moving forward. Taking that bit of extra time to be prepared is a good thing: be smart and move forward.

Knowing When to Move On

et's face it; if you have a job of any sort, you are better off than some people.

Plenty of good, hardworking folks are out of work or struggling to get by, living in a paycheck-to-paycheck state of existence, which is neither easy nor desired by anyone. But living safe only for the sake of being safe is not any way to live a life either.

Life and happiness are about a lot more than only money.

Humans must get satisfaction on a regular basis to enjoy their lives. This applies to jobs, relationships, and daily life. You can tolerate going to the events that you have no desire to be at, or you can put in several months working on a project that drains you.

The key is being able to recognize when too long is too much and then moving on. You can stick something out for only so long if you are not happy doing it.

The universe has a funny way of knowing when you are going through difficult times. Ever been in a bad mood and the radio plays a song that fits your mood? That is what I'm talking about.

Counter to this, though, is that even if the universe knows you need a change, it is going to help you only if you let it and the world around you know that you are ready for a change. Explaining the magic of the universe is not something I'm prepared to do at this time, but I will teach you some ways to leverage its magical ways.

Once you've realized that a change is needed, the first thing you should do is let the people closest to you know about the unhappiness and explain that this is more than a typical "I hate my job" moment that we all go through. Let them know that it is draining you and that a change is needed.

Rather than assuming that they are going to instantly help, you must ask directly for help in order to receive it. Assuming they know how much you need their assistance is a dangerous approach. When you need help, always ask for it.

Although friends want to help you, many don't want to feel like they are imposing on you by suggesting changes unless they are directly asked for their input.

Realizing that a change is needed is only the first step toward a happier life, and in many cases, it is the easiest one because all you need to do is accept that a change is needed and decide to move forward. Now the real work begins!

CHAPTER

5

The Power of
Writing It Down

 You should always have a small notebook on you.

I use Field Notes notebooks, but any small
notebook that fits in your pocket, purse, or
backpack will do. You should have it with you at
all times.

If you ever meet me, I can promise you that I'll have a notebook with me. It is a very rare occasion that I go out without having one with me. Sure, I have my phone and iPad with me and can make quick notes on those if I need to, but I find that nothing focuses me better or is quicker to go back and flip through than handwritten notes.

Once you have your notebook, be sure to put some form of contact information inside the front cover. I have yet to lose one, but I hope that if I did, whoever found it would take the few minutes to contact me; I can't imagine my scratches are going to do much for that person, so why would he or she want to keep it?

Another trick that I've learned over the years is to date each notebook as well. Inside the front cover or on the first page, write the date you start to use the notebook. When you get to the end, it is always fun to look back to see when you started it. Plus, if you save the notebooks (and you should), it makes keeping them in order much easier.

I have to give special thanks to two close friends who showed me the way of the notebook: motivator Julien Smith and multimedia storyteller

Clarence Smith Jr. were the first to push the idea into my head. We were sitting down over breakfast one morning when they started harping on the importance of always having one with you. If it wasn't for these two men, I'm not sure I would fully appreciate how important a notebook can play in someone's life. And I'm glad they pushed me to adopt it so that I can turn around and do the same to you.

There will be exercises throughout this book when you are encouraged to write in your notebook. Keep it handy as you continue to read. And remember, even after those exercises are done and you've finished reading this book, the power of writing down ideas, dreams, and goals in a notebook is an important one.

You can use your notebooks to jot down grocery lists, business ideas, or random doodles. Your notebook is a sacred place where no idea is a bad idea, so don't censor yourself. You never know when an idea might hit you, and it is always better to write it down than to forget it.

There is something very powerful about writing something down versus typing it into a device. It forces you to think about the words, there's no Delete key to hide the mistakes, and it's instantly more tangible.

Do me a favor, please. If you ever come to a book reading or other event I'm at, hold up your notebook and show it to me. We'll share a knowing nod and a smile. That would make my day.

The Three-Word Exercise

I first heard about this focusing exercise from blogger and author Chris Brogan. Since then, I've adopted the practice and added it to my end-of-year activities.

This exercise isn't dictated by any calendar, and it can be done at any time it is needed.

This will help you focus your thoughts and goals for anything. If you've got the yearning and need to make a shift, use it to focus on what are the most important things to you in a new job. Not in a great relationship? Perhaps this will help you figure out what you are truly looking for in a partner. Trying to decide what college to attend? Step through this to determine what's going to make it the most rewarding experience.

Although this can be used for anything, here I show how you can use it specifically to make a job change.

You can always make more money, but what you should focus on here are the important pieces—beyond the salary—that make you happy in a job. To come up with your three words do the following:

1. *Think about all the things you want to do in the coming year.* This includes both the small and the large. Take a week to really think about this, and in the notebook you have with you at all times, write down ideas as they come to mind. (You did get a notebook, right?) Don't worry about how you are going to accomplish

the items on your list or if they are really what you want to focus on or not; just write them all down.

2. *Once done, read through your notes.* Look for any themes that might cover multiple entries. Are there several locations or events listed? Roll those up into a travel theme. Talking about writing or other content you want to make, roll those up into a create theme. Not everything can be rolled up, but it is fairly common to have similar things that can be grouped together under a new word.

3. *Make note of the various themes that arise.* Since you can pick only three words to focus on, you must now take the time to think about which ones you want the most. To be successful, you can't have thoughts along the lines of, "Well, it would be cool if I . . ." You are picking three words that exemplify goals you are going to work toward achieving, so choose appropriately.

Although the first two steps are more brainstorming and analysis and can be completed quickly, this third step requires thought and introspection and is more difficult. If you are really committed to doing this and putting real thought into it, a certain level of introspection and analysis will happen here.

By the end of this step, you have will have whittled the list down to only three words. The last cuts will be the hardest, but you will be better off by having the focus narrowed down to only three words.

4. *Write down your words and share them with others*. By putting them out into the world, you are giving them life and letting others know they can help you achieve the goals behind them.

When I choose my words, I write a blog post to share them with others. Sharing them allows close friends to nudge you from time to time to see how you are doing with them.

Of course, it is up to you if you want to share them or not, but either way, be sure to write them down and keep them close so that you can look at them every so often. I like to print them out in large type and hang them up near my desk. It is hard to escape them when you do that.

Recently, when I stepped through this exercise, it looked like Figure 6.1.

Self

I've always been about helping others, and that will never change. But I realized I needed to focus on helping myself as well.

I'd like to grow old with my family and play with my grandkids. I've got too many places left to see and people left to hug in this world. I need to focus more on my health.

I also realized that I have to promote my work and myself more. It's a balancing act that each of us struggles with.

It also means not saying, "I'd like to . . . ," and then not going any further. This might refer to learning to play guitar, creating things with

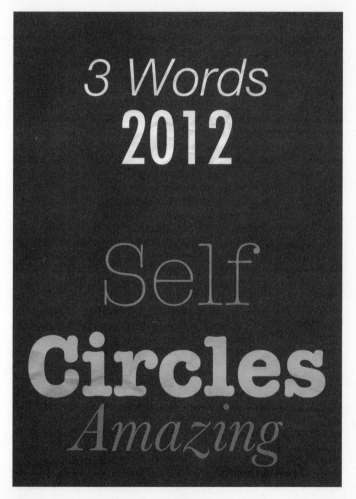

Figure 6.1   The poster I made for my office to remind me of the three words I chose.

my hands, or doing anything else I haven't made the time for.

Circles

Google got the metaphor correct that our lives are full of circles. Just like throwing a pebble into a pond, circles can grow and make other circles, but we are connected to groups of people. Some groups overlap; some are completely separate from other parts of our lives. But all are important.

Although you can stay connected to many relationships online, they also require face-to-face contact. Rather than depending on technology and social networks to connect, I am making sure I include more face-to-face time at events and making more time for calls and visits.

Amazing

When I first shared this word, I did not fully share publicly why I had chosen it. The reason for the word was because I knew that I'd be writing this book, and thus how could it not be one of my three words?

Yet it is more than that. It is about finding the amazing things in life and sharing in amazing experiences with those whom I love. It's about creating bits of amazement with the talents I've been given.

■ ■ ■

Choosing the three words is not easy, but this is a helpful exercise that will give you a guide for the year ahead and where you want to go next in life.

It can be done on a smaller scale as well. For example, you can choose one word for each month as a theme to focus on. This could be something as tactical as *cardio*, with the motivation of hitting the treadmill as many days as possible. Or it may be something more abstract, such as *smiles*, where you hope to be the impetus behind as many smiles as possible in the month through a variety of experiences and helpful moments.

Another version of the three-word exercise is the old-fashioned pro/con list. Although this can be a good starting point, such a list tends to focus more on details and tasks than on the bigger goals you have. Sure, a long commute is a con and a large salary is a pro, but does that help you find the right job? Would you take any job just because it is close to home and would give you a huge paycheck?

If you are more comfortable starting with a pro/con list, you can treat it like the big word list. As you write down more and more, you'll start seeing themes rise to the top.

As you come up with your three words, I welcome you to share them with me. I'd love to see what this inspires.

CHAPTER

The Magic of Turkey Pot Pie

C ooking is something I've loved doing my entire life. Cooking even simple meals can be therapeutic; your life will be much more fulfilling and satisfying if you know your way around a kitchen.

Many of the most important moments in life are in some way tied to food. Whenever there is something to celebrate, a reason to get together with friends or family, or even a time to mourn losses, food is involved.

There is a joke in my family that we may forget many details of a special memory, but we never forget what we ate. Every generation of Chapmans enjoy their food.

My favorite type of restaurant is a greasy spoon diner—the kind of place with polished chrome, seats at the counter, and a hardy menu of comfort foods. Although I always go for the corned beef hash and eggs (if it is homemade), today I want to talk about something else you'll find on the menu: turkey pot pie.

It's a simple combination of turkey, peas, carrots, and onions in a cream sauce that is either baked into a pastry pie shell or served over a biscuit. It is a simple, hearty, and filling dish. It warms you on a cold winter day and fills you up any time you order it. Simple, yet satisfying.

We're talking about food because as you look at what you want to do and how you want to move forward, you should keep in mind that it doesn't have to be something epic or flashy. Many people think that what they'd like to do is too niche or not exciting enough.

You need to focus on what *you* want to do.

Turkey pot pie is simple and not flashy, but people love it and pay for it. It leaves you with a satisfied feeling, and although it may not get a front-page review in *Gourmet* magazine, it still is an important menu item.

If what you want to do is simple yet satisfying, go for it.

Although it would be awesome to come up with the next great idea that gets funded and then bought by a bigger former start-up, that reality happens to only a small portion of us.

In his book, *The $100 Startup*, Chris Guillebeau gives examples of people who had a turkey pot pie idea and found success from it. The ideas included everything from selling mattresses to giving travel advice and even opening a yarn store. Each of them started with a small and simple idea that they grew into a successful business.

No greater example of this is the recent influx of food trucks.

They have swept across the world in recent years. Most of them serve only a few menu items, but what they serve is what they are best at.

Don't get hung up on your idea for a business not being big or flashy enough. The world is full of big and small everything, and we know that size doesn't matter if you know what you are doing.

People appreciate simple. Flashy may get attention, but you should be focusing on what people come back for.

Every day, around the country, people sit down and order turkey pot pie for that exact reason.

CHAPTER

Don't Let the Seagulls Get You Down

Think about the times you've been by the ocean watching the waves crash and felt the sand be sucked out from beneath your feet as the tides do their magical dance. You'll also see your fair share of seagulls and other birds flying around and making a hell of a racket.

Life (on the ocean or otherwise) is always going to be full of seagulls. You can spot them rather easily because they are constantly making noise, swooping in from time to time and shitting on you before flying away.

Real seagulls will leave a white mess on your head and shoulders, but people whom I refer to as seagulls are even more dangerous, because what they leave behind is self-doubt and uncertainties, both of which you must learn to ignore.

Managers, colleagues, and even clients can trigger these feelings. You've been working hard on an assignment, and someone says something along the lines of, "This isn't at all what we were looking for."

When this happens (and oh yes, it *will* happen), there are one of two responses:

1. Let the comment get you down and send you into a world self-doubt.

2. Consider what was said and, more important, who said it. Do a gut check to see how you

feel about the assigned tasks and then stand your ground.

You could also ignore the seagull completely and push forward. This one works only if the seagull in question is someone you've worked with for a long time and whose habits you know. Just be smart about your decision to ensure that you don't end up being disciplined in some manner.

You may run into seagulls the minute you start talking about making changes. Not everyone is going to agree with your thinking.

Parents and partners are the most likely candidates to become seagulls, but anyone could become one—and that can be dangerous, especially if the seagull is someone close to you whom you trust.

The key to dealing with people like this is to let them say what they are going to say. They are not going to go away until they get what they want. Just like that seagull that wants one of your fries, people have to dump what is on their mind or they might never move on.

Family and friends who do this to you are easy to deal with. Unless you live with them, this is your life, and that means you make the decisions. But, not everyone who challenges you is a seagull.

A seagull will dump and move on, but someone who actually cares about you and is questioning the logic will help you vet your decisions. You need to be challenged to make sure that what you are doing is really what you want. Although we may dream of making a big change, it isn't always the right time to do so.

You have to have confidence in the decisions you make. When you are confident in your ideas, the seagulls won't distract you from your goal. They can peck and scream all they want, but you can ignore them and push forward.

Simplify, Focus, and Attack

A few years ago, these were my three words. But beyond that exercise, they are three critical words that you need to keep in mind at all times.

Can three simple words really be that important?

Yes, because any question, issue, concern, or goal can be broken down using them. If it can't, then you don't want it bad enough or haven't taken the time to really determine how to get to it.

When setting goals, it often helps to break them down into smaller steps. This allows you to move forward more quickly with many small victories, instead of working only toward larger and further apart goals that take longer to achieve.

Simplify

Before making any major life adjustments, you have to know what in your life can be sacrificed and what can't.

Journalist Ellen McGirt, a senior writer for *Fast Company* magazine, told me, "You can't do it if you don't take good care of yourself. That means taking inventory of your obligations. Do you have children? Do you have rent? If you are not able to do it right now, then you set a plan in motion that helps you feel hopeful for when you can actually launch your plan without destroying the lives of others in the process."

As you look to simplify things, what is the bare minimum you and your family can tolerate? Think about income, time away from the family, and anything else that might change as you make a shift. You should never do anything that risks the happiness of the people who mean the most to you.

As you consider your goal, what are the intermediate steps that need to be taken in order to achieve it? It doesn't matter if you want to start your own company or completely shift gears; sit down and determine what tasks need to be achieved to make this goal a reality.

Simplify the end goal by breaking it down into attainable rungs you can climb to success.

Focus

Life is full of distractions, yet nothing is unobtainable when you fully focus on it.

How often have you logged on to check e-mail, and the next thing you know an hour (or more) has disappeared?

When we simplify our lives, it is much easier for our brains to focus on our goals. We are able to break larger goals into smaller tasks and focus on "losing 5 pounds in one week," rather than "fitting into a bikini by July."

There is nothing wrong with having big dream goals, but they are much harder to achieve because they are sometimes pie in the sky, life lists sort of goals that we'd love to get to someday but can't focus directly on at this time.

It is best to minimize distractions as much as possible and schedule time every week when you put diversions and obligations aside and work on creating and executing a plan to reach your goals.

This is as simple as a change of scenery. Go for a walk. Take your laptop to a coffee house. Get away from the day-to-day tasks around you so that you can focus on the future.

If the Internet is the main thing getting in the way of your focus, there is an app named Freedom that can help with that. You can tell it how many minutes you want to be free from the Internet; it gives you exactly what you asked for.

Once you hit okay, the only way to get on the Internet is to reboot your computer.

Never forget that the key to maintaining your focus is to cut down on the distractions. The better you get at that, the more amazing things that will happen for you.

Attack

You've simplified your list and have your mind focused on your goals. Now what?

Now you get to do the work and go make your goals a reality.

Stop waiting for permission or some sign that it is the right time. If you've gotten to this point, it *is* the time. Plus, I'm a firm believer that it is always better to ask for forgiveness than permission.

Soldiers never go into battle blindly, and neither should you. Make an attack plan. Figure out what strategies are best and then go forth and kick ass!

CHAPTER

10

Everyone Has Excuses

We all make excuses about what's holding us back from chasing our dreams:

"I'm not a twenty-something. I can't just throw caution to the wind."

"I've got a mortgage to pay, kids to feed, and too many responsibilities."

"I'm too young to do anything of meaning."

"I don't live in a thriving area, and I can't move."

Excuses are a dime a dozen, and most likely there is some merit to each of them.

All people who achieve greatness have doubts. At some point they made excuses, but the difference is that they stopped making them and decided to take action to reach their goals.

If you just thought something along the lines of, "I don't know if I can," that's the normal reaction.

The key lesson that you must learn is that although making excuses may be human nature, people who live their dream life learn to stop making them. An excuse is nothing more than a self-imposed roadblock.

Life is going to put up enough challenges for you; you don't need to add any more into the mix. They serve no purpose. Buckle down and embrace that it's natural to be concerned and have self-doubt but remember that making excuses helps no one.

11

No More Saying, "I Can't"

These two simple words—"I can't"—have the power to hold people back from achieving their dreams. But there is very little that you can't do if you work hard enough and long enough.

"I can't" is the mental block that we use to convince ourselves that it is okay to give up.

GORUCK is a lifestyle brand that makes a variety of rucksacks and other equipment. The company also hosts the GORUCK Challenge, which it markets as 10 to 13 hours of "good living."

In reality it is a grueling half-day of physical punishment that will test you to your limits. If you imagine boot camp crammed into half of a day, you have an idea of what it might be like.

Of the challenge, Jason McCarthy, founder and chief executive officer of GORUCK, says, "The biggest challenge to overcome is your own mind. Yes, there are physical challenges, but the hardest ones are all in your head."

I share this example because Jason is a seasoned Green Beret and now a successful businessman. He is also one of the happiest people I've ever met, because when he decided his dream was to build a successful brand, he knew that he couldn't let himself say, "I can't," and not push forward.

You have to be dedicated to the goal and want it more than anything. Saying, "I can't," is dangerous because it shows you are not dedicated enough. It is an easy excuse people use to escape doing whatever it is they are being asked to do. It is the easiest out.

What people really mean most of the time is, "I won't": I won't put in the hard work. I won't put in the hours it is going to take to achieve my goals. I won't push myself harder than I've ever been pushed because I'm scared.

Think about what is standing in your way of achieving whatever it is you want to do next. Write them all down in your notebook, leaving a space under each. If you really want a new life, then you've got to think of *everything* in your way—it may be a long list.

Once you complete your list, consider each item. Below each one, write down what it would take to eliminate that one as a roadblock. What is it going to take to clear every single roadblock out of the way so that you can continue down the path to amazing things?

Many of them won't be easy to clear. If you want to make a big shift career-wise and you have a family, it is instantly harder for you. (Sometimes being single does have its advantages, but I'd still never trade those for my loving kids and wife.) You just must find a way to balance it all and make your new goals work with your current life situation.

People every day tell themselves that they can't do certain things. They worry about what others will think and say. But the only person standing in your way is you. If we haven't been true to our desires and dreams, then what was the point?

Shouldn't you be able to do everything you want? People stand in their own way every day, and I've never understood that. You owe it to yourself to get out of your own way and chase your dreams.

Change is never easy for anyone, but you need to face it to be happy.

We all have friends who have come to us in one of these situations. They always have a list of reasons they can't make a change for the better. The next time it happens, really listen to what they are saying and think about how many of their reasons have actual merit and how many are just excuses they are making so that they don't have to face change.

The next time you catch yourself saying, "I can't," stop immediately.

Think about why you said it and what it really means. If you did it, would anyone be hurt? If you did it, what would ultimately be at risk, and what is the worst thing that could happen? If the answers to those questions come back with nothing drastic, tell the person you thought about it some and you will give it a try.

The first time doing anything is hard. But you'll feel better after doing it!

CHAPTER
12

Stop Talking; Start Doing

We all do it. We talk more than we do.
No matter what the task is, talking about
how you are going to do it is always easier than
actually getting it done. You have to do the work.

The creative team members at Nike who came
up with the slogan of "Just Do It" were geniuses.

Those three words strung together are at once powerful, simple, and motivating. Of course, the talkers will hear that and say something like, "I would just do it, but . . . ," and then throw in one of a multitude of excuses of why they can't do it right now.

Author, speaker, and marketing expert Seth Godin believes you should "always be shipping." Successful people are doers. They don't just talk about a big project they want to do or the book they want to write. They get it done, and they ship it out the door.

In your notebook, write down five things you'd love to do. Not big crazy bucket list items, but five things that you really want to accomplish in the near future.

Really look at them and think about what is standing in the way of getting them done. We're not talking about life-changing goals like we were earlier, but rather smaller items or tasks that you'd find satisfaction in completing soon.

Not enough time and not enough money are not valid reasons. Yes, depending on what you'd like to accomplish, they are valid concerns. But if they truly are the only items preventing you from doing what you want to do, then you should find a way to make more of both. Determined individuals will always find a way if they want it bad enough.

Now below each goal, list the four or five obstacles that would need to be overcome or steps that would have to occur to make each one happen. Perhaps you need more knowledge around how to do something, or maybe you need to find someone with a special skill set. By breaking down these items, you've begun to pull together a to-do list and a plan.

Next, rank each item on your list from easiest to hardest to complete. Take in consideration everything that would go into fully making them happen and be successful.

Look at your original list again and rank them in order of importance to you. Figure out which one would give you the most satisfaction and would make you the happiest to complete.

Compare the two ranked lists. Is there any pattern? Are any of the easy-to-complete ones also ones that would give you the most satisfaction? Why not go after those immediately then? Nothing wrong with small, quick, and awesome victories.

We all have dream lists of things we'd love to do someday, and because there is limited time and always competing priorities, we have to decide which items to pursue and which will hang on our dream board or life list.

Picking what you focus your time and energy on is critical. Too many people will try to work on multiple projects at one time, and this always means that at least one project suffers. Focus on one item and make it happen. An undivided mind is a focused mind, and when the mind is focused, that's when things get done.

If you always have more than one iron in the fire, it may lead you down a more difficult path. And with less attention on many goals, it may take you longer to complete just one.

On the converse side, for now, forget about those that are the hardest to complete and the lowest on your satisfaction level—you can add them to your golden ticket list described later.

The key factor is to realize that amazing things come only to those who work hard at making them happen. Getting to work and putting in the long hours to make your dreams come true is the only way goals are achieved.

13

Risk Can Be Scary; Embrace It and Move Forward

Humans are programmed to run away from things that scare them. The flinch instinct is there to save us from threats or danger.

In his book *The Flinch*, author Julien Smith explains, "Your flinch has become your worst enemy. It should be a summoning, a challenge to push forward. Instead, the challenge is getting refused. . . . If you refuse to face the flinch, it means the fear is choking you."

The greater the risk, the sweeter the victory. But at the same time, completely throwing caution to the wind isn't a smart move either.

The trick is that you have to figure out how much risk is acceptable in your current situation. Changing jobs if you're a 22-year-old with no commitments has a very different level of associated risk than if you're a 42-year-old with a spouse and kids. Every situation is different, but life is filled with risks. And the older we get, the more scared we become of it.

Think back to some of the stupid things you did as a kid. How many trees did you jump out of, how many after-dark activities did you take part in, and how many risky adventures did you go on? When we are young, we understand risk, but we also are more accepting of leaning into it rather than flinching and avoiding it.

Part of that is getting wiser as we grow older, but at the same time most people in the world are getting more scared as they get older.

If you want to chase your dreams and live the life you've always wanted, it comes with risk. As you look out toward your future, it's natural to be a bit scared, because you don't know definitively if it is all going to work or not.

Stop and look at where you were five years ago. Would you have predicted you'd be where you are and accomplished what you have? How much of where you are was part of a master plan?

What can help diffuse, or at least reduce, risk is having an accurate understanding of exactly what risks are associated with making a change in your life. Only by being aware of them can you create a plan to reach your goals that gives you the best chance for success.

Risk scares everyone. Those who embrace the fear and push forward are the ones who will find success. No one who has obtained success and happiness wasn't scared of the risk. Acknowledge it and then push forward.

14

Quitting Is Always an Option

I can't sit here and tell you that quitting is something that you should never do.

I know every coach I've ever had would cringe if they read that, but I'm a realist and I know the difference between a game and life. They are not always one and the same, and no matter how hard we fight, each of us will quit more than once in our lives.

Seth Godin talks at length about this in his classic book *The Dip*. He shares numerous stories and bits of advice on why you need to realize that, if you are stuck in the dip and may never get out, you should quit. I list it as one of my "dangerous" books in the Appendix because it could open your eyes to the fact that you might be in a dip in your current situation.

This may seem to contradict my advice to never say, "I can't," but in fact these are at the opposite ends of the decision cycle. If you never start something, you can never quit. Once you've moved past telling yourself you couldn't do something, you'll begin doing it. But what if you realize you can never finish it?

The hardest part about quitting anything is that you'll never know what the outcome would have been. The questions and regrets can eat at you for the rest of your life. What if you had stuck it out a few months longer or put in an extra hour a day of harder work to try and make it a success? These are not questions you should focus on.

Instead, if you are in the middle of something and your heart is no longer in it, then you have grounds to consider quitting.

The key thing with quitting is to do it as quickly as possible once the decision has been made. Dragging it out and not making a swift transition gives you time to change your mind—or gives others time to make it up for you.

Never forget that every situation is different, and people will have varying outside factors that must be thought about. It doesn't matter if it is a relationship or a job; quitting anything comes with consequences, so be sure to think about those before making your decision.

Everyone decides to make changes in their lives for different reasons. It is up to you to really look into your heart and determine when is the right time to make your change. It is never easy, clean, or without consequences. But if it is the right thing to do, you'll look back and be thankful you made the decision.

15

Know What You Hate and Then Don't Do It

Take a moment and think about the tasks in your life that you truly hate. Not the ones that you don't like, because there will always be those, but rather the ones that you completely dread doing.

By thinking only of the things that you really hate, you can consider the possibility that there are other ways these tasks can be done without you spending time doing them. There may be things you don't love to do, but they are far from appearing on your hate-to-do-them list.

As you make the transition in life to being happier, you need to figure out what these tasks are for you and immediately figure out a way to have someone else do them.

This is difficult to do for most people because it involves having trust that whomever is chosen to do it will do it properly. Delegation is one of the scariest things in life, yet you must do it to save your sanity.

The other issue is one of cost. Hiring an accountant or gardener or having your spouse fold the laundry all comes with a cost.

Flip your thinking around for a minute.

Although it may cost you money (or favors in the case of the laundry), if you truly hate the task, isn't it worth it? What is the cost on your happiness to doing it yourself and hating every moment of it?

Get out your notebook and make a list of things you don't like doing. Don't narrow it down or think twice. Brain dump onto the pages everything that comes to mind for the next 15 minutes.

Once you've got a complete list, think about which ones you dread the most and which take time away from the things you enjoy. As you analyze and play one against the other, you'll realize that some are despised more than others.

Circle the ones that are the most dreaded. Make sure you select a combination of business and personal tasks, because we all have both. Try to limit the most dreaded tasks to a maximum of five. As you look at the circles, think, "Well, that one I can deal with if I have to, but this one makes me want to scream." Keep the screamers on the list.

Now think of ways you can get those tasks done without having to do them yourself. You can bet that for most tasks you hate, there is someone you can hire to do them for you. Don't have the money to hire a bookkeeper yet? Perhaps you can barter a trade or come up with another unique solution. But, even if you do need to pay someone to do the most hated of the tasks, it is so worth it if it means saving your sanity!

16

With a Little Help from Our Friends

If you want to go fast, go alone. If you want to go far, go together.

—African Proverb

No one can be successful solely on his or her own.

There are different levels of friendship, but the friends who will help you achieve your goals are the ones who really matter in life. Having a large social graph certainly can help you achieve your goals, but your inner circle of friends are the ones who will challenge, encourage, and support you the most.

When you set off on something challenging and amazing, you are not going to be able to do it alone. The Beatles had it right when they sang, "with a little help from my friends."

Sure, you can go it alone and try to push through everything, but your chances of succeeding are greatly diminished if you do. Asking for help can be awkward, but friends would rather you ask than see you fail. Always keep that in mind.

This doesn't mean cashing in every favor or depending on your friends to do the work for you, because that isn't going to be successful either. You've still got to do the work, and they will help you where they can—but only if you ask them specifically for help.

And remember, help comes in many flavors. Different friends can provide different types of help to you, and you'll only learn this by asking for help and over time.

Stop for a moment and think about everything you are hoping to accomplish. Which of your friends might be able to assist in the smallest of ways?

Write it all down in your notebook, specifying what type of help you are hoping to get from each friend. Some might possess a certain skill that you need. Others will know someone that you'd like an introduction to. However each person can be an asset to you, write it down so that you don't forget to reach out to each friend individually.

You cannot be afraid to ask for help. People want to help others, and if they even remotely care about you, then they will be glad to step up and help you with anything you ask for, if they can.

Never assume that they know what you need them to do. Just because you mention that you are looking for a new job doesn't mean they are going to think to introduce you to people. If you want something specific done by your friends, then come right out and say exactly what sort of help you are looking for.

If you never ask, you'll never receive.

CHAPTER

17

Life Is Too Short for Bad Wine

The concept of collecting wine is something that I've never fully understood. Isn't drinking wine more fun than looking at a dusty bottle on a shelf?

Right now, I have many bottles of wine in our basement. When my wife and I took a vacation to Napa Valley, we ended up shipping home several cases of our favorite new discoveries. Ever since that vacation, we've had a surplus since we tend to only drink it when we have friends or family over. We want to enjoy it, but bought more than we can drink on our own.

Ric Elias, a passenger on Flight 1549 when it crash-landed in the Hudson River, gave an inspiring TED talk called "3 Things I Learned While My Plane Crashed." He talks about how he wants to collect only bad wine, because he wants to make sure that any time he is with friends, he is drinking the good stuff. He wants to make sure that he has nothing but great times and experiences with every person in his life. His take on living is inspiring, and he certainly has a reason to share it.

Call it carpe diem, call it making the most of your time on earth, but the truth is that no one knows how long he or she is going to live or when his or her last day is going to arrive. It is a sad thought, but it is the truth, and we can't yet escape it.

Any day you are not sick and are above ground is a good day. It is a simple reminder, but one that bears repeating. Keep it in mind on those mornings when you wake up and don't want to get out of bed.

Knowing this, why not do what you love? Why wouldn't you open up the bottle of red that you've been saving for when your friends come over to dinner? Why settle for slaving away at a job you are not happy at when you have a dream to be something else? What is keeping you from doing that one thing you've always thought about but have yet to do?

Sometimes you have to slave away to take care of your commitments, but long term, will that give you the life you want? When you close your eyes for the last time, you are certainly not going to look back and wish you had punched the clock for a few more hours of overtime.

Of course, this speaks to more than just your career. So many people say they dream about visiting a far off country, trying a new activity, or devoting time to something they love. They talk about it as if it is impossible to do immediately. And although you might have to save up for that epic trip or schedule some time off to focus on a new hobby, stop talking about it and collecting all those dreams on a shelf or on a to-do list.

It's good to have a list, but only as long as you are regularly checking items off the list as often as possible. Only dreaming about a list is as bad as collecting wine instead of drinking it.

Why create a list of any sort if the goal is not to check off as many as possible?

Life is short, and you have only a set number of years, days, and minutes to do what you really want to do. Stop thinking about what you want to do and go out and do it.

Maybe uncorking that bottle of wine you've been saving for a special day is the perfect way to get started.

CHAPTER
18

Be a Duck

It doesn't matter what industry you work in, where you live in the world, or how positive your outlook on life is. The fact of the matter is that there are going to be days, events, and people who are going to drive you nuts.

We've all had that boss, teacher, friend, acquaintance, or partner who drives us crazy. No matter how hard we work, it's never enough.

No matter how many good ideas we present, they are never quite enough or aren't good enough. These situations can be an energy drain and motivation killer.

There are people in our lives who, no matter how much we love them, act in ways that upset us. Maybe you have one of those people in your life who is a constant doubter. Or a pessimist who constantly sees the world as never getting better.

Since we can't get rid of them, we've got to learn to live with them.

You've got to accept that none of those people are going to change. They are not going to go away either.

The way you are going to survive this is by being a duck.

Ever watch ducks in a pond? They swim around without a care in the world. Have you noticed what they do when it starts raining? Most ducks will keep on swimming; they are already in the water after all. They keep on swimming as if nothing has changed.

This is what I mean when I tell you to be a duck.

When the bad situations arise and you want to scream or give up, you have to be like those ducks and let the problems roll off you like water. Ducks can't do anything about the rain that falls, and by recognizing that fact, they keep on with their lives. They know that it will always be part of their lives and keep pushing forward.

Some problems are harder than others to let wash off us, but this mentality is for the day-to-day guff that we have to put up with.

The key to this being successful for you is the acceptance factor.

I once worked for a company that had great potential, the funding to succeed, and a stable of talent working with them. Over and over, others and myself would show them how, with small changes and different actions, they could become the company we all dreamed it would become. Since I had nothing to lose, I was very vocal with my constructive criticisms, but I was also very forth-coming with practical advice and suggestions.

I was told that I should stop my approach because people were starting to label me a "nagging Nelly."

I realized that whereas I saw what I was doing as helping, the people in power saw it as only nagging. They had their way of doing things and were not going to deviate from it no matter what it meant. Even though they had surrounded themselves with a group of some of the brightest and most creative people in the industry, they merely wanted them to be blind minions instead of true partners.

From that point forward, I decided that I'd approach this situation like a duck would.

When they made a decision that I didn't agree with, I sort of shrugged my shoulders and ignored it. Unless it directly affected me or others I cared about in a negative way, I no longer got angry about decisions that I knew I had zero chance of making better. (I did keep an eye on things so that I could steer clear as needed, though.)

Yes, it was hard at times to do this because I had invested so much time and passion into the success I believed we could have, but the bitter pill of reality was one I had to swallow. And you too will have to sometimes.

Letting it wash over you like water might come naturally for a duck, but it isn't that easy to do as a human. The more passionate we are about something, the harder it is to face situations that we are not happy with.

It does get easier as you let more decisions wash over you. And it comes in handy when dealing with teenagers and coworkers alike.

Be aware that this response can upset some people as well.

People may think that you are giving up or not fighting hard enough. They are right; that's exactly what you are doing. What they don't realize is that you are just smarter about the battles you pick to fight and that you know that there is no sane reason to mount an attack when there is zero chance of winning.

As we've discussed, knowing when to quit is equally important as knowing when to fight. When the best option is not to, that is when you have to embrace being a duck.

This is why you have to be careful about shaking your duck feathers in public or in front of the people who are forced to think this way in the first place. Worse than being tagged as the complainer is being tagged as the complacent one.

The next time it seems that things are out of control around you, that you can't change it no matter what you do, remember a duck in the rain.

Quack! Quack!

CHAPTER

19

To Each Their Own . . .

G rowing up, my father said this to me quite often.

He was reminding me that I wouldn't always agree with what people said or did and that although I may not agree with it, if it wasn't hurting anyone, I shouldn't waste my energy fighting them on it.

Not everyone around you is going to share the same beliefs or values as you do. The sooner you accept this, the better your life will be. Remembering that can keep you sane when you see people doing, saying, and sharing things that you don't agree with.

Internet users as a whole could use a lesson in this. There is no reason you have to comment on every post you see and don't agree with. Sure, if you have something constructive to add to the conversation, then go forth and add your thoughts. But if you have nothing more than a "Do you know how wrong you are?" or "I don't agree," is it worth your time?

This isn't a trick question. The answer is no.

One of the great things about the human race is that we are each entitled to our own opinions and beliefs. This means that we won't always agree, and many times our own beliefs will differ from those around us.

There is no reason that you have to go head to head with those who think differently than you. In fact, being exposed to a variety of beliefs is a good thing. It makes you a more rounded individual.

Civil debate around ideas is a healthy activity. Too often people fall into the trap of arguing and pointing fingers. This helps no one, and if you are the one raising your voice for no reason, people will remember.

Try to keep an even keel always in your life. This can become especially hard concerning religion, politics, and favorite sport teams. It is even harder when those around you are the types who have to go on the offensive with those who don't share their particular beliefs.

Life is more enjoyable when you focus on the good in your life rather than on those you disagree with.

The next time someone does or says something you don't agree with, if it doesn't affect you, the best thing to do to avoid unnecessary conflict might be to remember, "To each their own."

Forget Skipping Pebbles; Throw a Boulder!

There are two kinds of people in this world: ocean lovers and lake lovers. If you stop and think about yourself, you likely fall into one of those camps and know people who fall into the other. Granted, there is nothing wrong with loving both of them.

Do you love going to the beach and watching the waves crash? Or do you prefer to listen to the lap of water against a wooded shoreline of a lake?

It's important to get outside and take in as much nature as possible. It might not help you achieve all your dreams, but it'll certainly make you happier. You'd be amazed at how happy a good dose of fresh air can make you.

An ocean is always in motion; it never stops. The waves ebb and flow every day and night. A lake or pond is still most of the time.

Think about the world around you right now. There are plenty of things that feel like the ocean. No matter what you do, you can't seem to make even a ripple in it. The waves keep coming and going, and no matter how hard you try to contain them, you can't.

But, if you are going to make changes, then you must find the calm bits of the world that you can disturb for your own benefit.

Being a dad means I've had the pleasure of teaching my children how to skip rocks. You have done this, right? Pick up the flattest, smoothest rock and with a sideways flick of your wrist, release it and watch as it magically skips across the water before sinking into the drink forever.

There is something beautiful in the simplicity of counting the skips and then doing it again and hoping for more.

The pastime of skipping stones is a great analogy to how many people live their lives. The natural inclination is to start out with a small pebble to see what it does. Then you find larger rocks to throw into the water. Those won't go very far, but you can bet when they hit the water there will be a huge splash.

Now take this concept and think about what you are working on and what you want to do. You, of course, want to share the news with others, and although you could certainly come forth meekly and tell the world immediately, perhaps that is not the best decision. Chucking a pebble out may get you a few skips, but what if you held off and worked harder to do something bigger for more of an impact?

As you plot the next steps of your life, start thinking about how to make the biggest impact. There is a lot to be said for mixing up what you do.

Take out your notebook and open it so that you are looking at two blank pages. On the top of the left-hand page, write "Pebbles," and on the right-hand page, write "Boulders." Write down all the ideas you could carry out in each column.

It is expected that you'll find yourself with more pebbles than boulders. Just like at any shoreline, it is easier to find rocks to skip than ones to make a big splash. But even though there are only so many boulders out there, make sure you find and use a few of them!

Living the Road Less Traveled

The classic poem by the great New England poet Robert Frost, "The Road Less Traveled," tells us that there are rewards in choosing a path not taken by most.

Living your life on the road less traveled is never easy. It will be covered in plenty of things to trip you up and block your progress. There will be days when you don't know what is around the next corner or where exactly you may be heading, and that can be unsettling to some.

Many people take the easy and well-worn path and go on to have fulfilling lives. There is no shame in taking the safe path, but there are often more surprises and opportunities on the other.

Yes, family, work, and other obligations will get in the way of your dreams, but those are excuses. Never forget that we each have the same 24 hours every day. No one gets any more or less time. It is up to you do with it what you want.

Remaining adventurous is a trait for success. Embracing your inner wanderlust to explore opportunities that may be ahead, even though you don't know exactly what obstacles you may face, often will fill your belly with nervousness—a nervousness that some of us find exciting.

Too many proceed through life without truly living it. Adding a bit of adventure and wonder into your life is never a bad decision.

When a chance to experience something new presents itself to you, don't make excuses as to why you can't or won't experience it. It doesn't matter if it is tasting a strange food, visiting an exotic destination, or trying a completely new activity. Every new experience makes you a better person. You should strive to always experience as much as you can in life.

Keep this in mind as you move forward with your new life. The path is rarely a straight line between today and when you reach your goals. It is common for there to be detours and sidetracks. Rather than being annoyed or nervous about these, take them for what they are and embrace them.

You never know what new opportunities, friendships, and possibilities lie around the next corner or will present themselves as a result of the decisions you make.

Suck it up. Focus and get out there. Live it. And never, ever give up.

This path is the fun one!

22

Focus on the Flame

Christopher S. Penn is a marketing writer and cofounder of PodCamp. Every year he holds a special New Year's celebration at his house. There are no noisemakers, champagne, or loud music.

Instead, it is a small group of close friends sitting in front of his fireplace, holding sticks and bowls of leaves and spending quiet quality time together.

This celebration is a goma-kan, or fire cere-mony. Chris explained that goma-kan "has its roots deep in Asian cultures and lore, stretching from Japan all the way back to the Himalayas, and is a powerful means of helping us focus on what we want to achieve and what conditions, internal and external, stand in our way of success."

Every year there is someone new at the cer-emony, and you can tell that this person doesn't know what's coming. Most people don't make the time for quiet moments of awesome such as this in their lives. More people should.

Although the details of the ceremony must remain secret, the end goal I can share with you. It boils down to being able to focus on the flame of your idea and goal. By sharing our goals with the fire, it gives us a focus point, something to think about, to picture in our minds, and to bring us back to what we need to do throughout the year.

Chris is a showcase example of someone who is constantly learning and, more important, openly sharing what he learns with others.

"I host it every year because it's important to me to share the knowledge my teachers have given me," says Chris. "Things like the goma-kan, if people commit to their goals, make the world a better place. Happier, healthier, more successful friends means that the people I choose to be around are bringing more lightness, more brightness to their worlds, which in turn brightens up mine. I repay the kindness my teachers have given me by paying it forward and conducting the exercise."

Every day we each are dealing with a swarm of distractions. There is no shortage of things begging for our attention. This makes it very easy to lose sight of our goals.

Although you may not take part in a goma-kan, you can still use its teachings to keep focused. Whenever you feel a bit lost or distracted, quiet yourself and concentrate on your goals. Take a few moments to close your eyes and really focus on what you want to achieve next.

Life moves quickly, and you will become distracted. Always find a way to balance the craziness out with some calmness to help you maintain your focus.

Learning to Say No

With only two letters, you'd think it would be one of the easiest words in the world to say, but the truth is, when opportunities start knocking, it can be one of the hardest. We've already discussed why you shouldn't be saying, "I can't," all the time, but that doesn't mean you say yes to everything either.

Once you achieve a certain level of success and are known by more than the people inside your house or cubicle, people will begin to approach you for help. This may come in the form of them wanting to buy you lunch, asking for a quick call, or the always fun picking of your brain. In the office, it sometimes gets masked with invites to committee meetings, closed-door conversations, or offers to buy you coffee.

The type of things you might have to say no to will, of course, depend on what line of work you are in. Perhaps you are always getting asked for free business advice, to look at business plans, or to give your opinion on a variety of topics. It is flattering every time because it means that people respect your thoughts, but it is also taking time away from the other tasks you should be focusing on.

You must learn to set boundaries and expectations.

No matter what your field of expertise, once you start living the life you want to live and doing the sort of work you've always dreamed about, people will come to you expecting a yes for an answer as the default.

When someone comes to you looking for a favor, ask yourself if you have the time. What will you have to sacrifice in order to do it? Will something you are striving for be pushed aside in order to complete it? If so, then you must ensure that it is worth it.

Perhaps you believe you should drop everything and anything for family or a close friend. That should go without saying.

You should strive to help as many people as you can in life. Cyberpunk futurist Eric Rice once told me, "Learn everything you can and share everything you know." That simple sentence is a good way to think about what you learn and what you choose to share.

The delicate balance you need to find, though, is between doing a favor to help someone and openly giving away your expertise and time for free to those whom you shouldn't.

When someone asks you for help, try to respond and help. In today's world, it sometimes takes only a few minutes to reply to an e-mail, and it takes even less time to respond to a text message or tweet. If the help that is being requested is as simple as that, you should always do it. Call it Karma or the Golden Rule; either way it makes sense in life to help others.

If it is more involved than that, you must look at everything on your plate and determine whether you have the time to take on more.

Your most valuable asset is time. You have only a finite amount of it to use every day. Like most people, you could use more hours in the day, but since you are limited to the time you have, be sure you are using it wisely.

The only way you are ever going to get others to value your time is if you value it first. You should never be afraid to ask for money in exchange for your knowledge and help. This is not to say that you should never do it for free (see previous discussion), but no matter how minimal of a life you live, you need money—we all do. And if you spend all your time doing work for free, you will run into financial issues.

When faced with one of these situations, think about what the recipient is going to get out of you saying yes. If you are asked to speak at a sponsored event and people are being charged to attend, there should be a budget to pay you for your time. When your services are desired by another company to help it grow and prosper, the company should understand that you need to do the same thing. It doesn't matter if you are a bookkeeper, photographer, or interior decorator. Everyone's time is valuable.

Musician, entrepreneur, and eternal good guy Derek Sivers believes that when presented with any request you shouldn't look at it as a yes or no question. You are either turned on enough to say "Hell Yeah" or you say no. This is a great test to put into practice the next time you are on the fence about what your answer should be.

Each case is going to be different, and after a few times of saying yes to something that ends up taking up more time and effort than you ever imagined or that your heart wasn't really into, you'll start being a bit more cautious.

But this is an issue bigger than just dollars and sense. It is about your peace of mind as well.

The more you say yes, the more tasks you are committed to getting done. Saying no and missing out on something is much better than saying yes and dropping the ball on successfully finishing it.

You must learn to be able to say, "I'd love to help you, but I've got a lot on my plate and unfortunately I can't assist you right now."

Whenever you have to say this, try to have someone you can recommend who might be able to help the person. If you don't have anyone immediately in mind, at least ask the person if it would help him or her to have some recommendations from you. This shows that you do want to help, even if you can't do it directly.

People understand that we all become busy, and they will respect you for replying promptly and politely. If they don't, read Chapter 31, which covers asshats and ankle biters.

If you value your time and want to live life to the fullest, you must learn to say no to things that won't help you progress forward. As with most things, it gets easier the more times you say it.

CHAPTER

24

Have a Small-Town Mentality

There are small towns in every corner of the world. Although the languages spoken, religions practiced, and foods eaten may be completely different, the deep-rooted approach to life of the people who live in them will always be the same.

As the Internet became more social, the world became smaller. Suddenly each of us could talk to, interact, and do business with anyone in the world. Borders no longer matter when it comes to friendships. The world has become one big small town.

Happy people come from small towns. I firmly believe that a lot of my core values come from growing up in a small town.

Now, don't worry if you grew up in a bustling city, because having a small-town mentality comes from inside rather than from what is around you. It is a compass to guide you in decisions and how you interact with people.

What are some small-town traits that everyone should adopt?

Always Say, "Good Morning"

Anyone who follows me online knows that I start most mornings with some form of greeting, wishing everyone a good morning. If we cross paths as I'm walking down the street, I'm just as likely to look you in the eyes and say, "Good morning." It is a simple greeting between strangers and friends, but it goes a long way.

Don't be bothered when someone doesn't say, "Good morning" or "Hello," back; it is just the way that person is and it's nothing to get upset over. When a smile crosses someone's face and that person replies with a reciprocating good morning, you'll understand the power of this type of thinking.

This can be boiled down to the simple fact that people like other friendly people. But how does someone know if you are friendly or not? They either develop the opinion by interacting with you or by listening to what other people say about you.

Every single person you meet face to face or virtually is constantly developing an opinion about you. The friendlier you are, the better that opinion will be.

Talk to Strangers

I can't tell you how many church suppers I went to with my grandmother growing up. There is nothing like a church basement full of elderly people you don't know to scare you as a little kid. Being around strangers is an awkward feeling for anyone at any age, yet if you embrace the fact that it is strange for everyone, you can use it to your advantage.

I learned that if I walked up to almost anyone at these events and said, "Hi, I'm Joyce's grandson," I'd get a smile back and a conversation would ensue. Suddenly, the person sitting next to me warmed up, and we were no longer strangers because we had my grandmother in common. The awkwardness would slowly fade away. Plus, they learned I liked chocolate cream pie, and at every future church supper, there would be one waiting for me.

The next time you are standing in line for your morning caffeine injection, say hello to the person in front of you. Sitting in a room waiting for a meeting to start? Turn to your neighbor and introduce yourself.

The only way you are going to meet new people is by saying hello to a stranger. Every day you'll be presented with opportunities to do this, and it is up to you to initiate it.

Please keep in mind that some people won't welcome your openness. Respect this and move on. The last thing you want to be is overly friendly. If the person replies and seems to be into it, then keep it up. If it is obvious the person is not in the mood, move on. Not everyone was meant to live in a small town.

Learn People's Names and Then Use Them

The small-town part of this comes from knowing the people behind the counter at the deli, on the other side of the window at the bank drive-through, and at the cash register at the grocery store. This instantly forms a level of trust between you and them. You are no longer doing business with a big company but directly with Mark, Peter, or Becky.

Businesses can learn a big lesson from this. People like to do business with companies that produce a good product at a fair price, but they also like to do business with people they know.

If you are trying to be more engaged online, give people a face and a name to get to know you better. Put your employees out there and let them build that trust for you.

For example, Scott Monty is the global head of social media for the Ford Motor Company. To the online world at large, he has become the face of Ford. He is not the only face, but a lot of people feel like they know him and can now talk to Ford because they can talk to Scott.

He interacts directly with individuals, and although he is professionally representing the company, he also allows his personal side to shine through as well. If a company as large as Ford can do this, so can you.

Develop a Reputation

Remember in high school when your parents told you that you didn't want to develop a reputation? But did you ever notice they always assumed that it would be a bad reputation?

I have a reputation of being a teddy bear of a nice guy. It comes in especially handy when it makes people who are currently adversaries drop their guard against me, but we'll save those evil stories for another book perhaps.

In today's world, everyone seems to know everyone else's business.

Whenever possible, you need to be ensuring that you are building the reputation you want. This isn't anything you can directly control, though, because people are going to form opinions about you based on all of your actions. Mess up one little thing, and it can tarnish your reputation. But couldn't you also bring it back to a shine by making several better decisions?

You can think about your reputation as a playground seesaw. It can be difficult to keep it balanced and in the middle. Lean too far in one direction, and it crashes down in that direction. But several small movements in both directions keeps it even and level.

Big things might have an immediate sweep in one direction, but your reputation is something that is constantly ebbing and flowing as you live your life.

Help Your Neighbor

Little gestures go a long way in life.

When we moved into our new house, several neighbors came by to welcome us. One had baked a loaf of zucchini bread, and another had picked grapes to add to the basket. It wasn't something they had bought at a store. Instead it showed that they had given us thought and cared enough to make it a personal welcome basket.

Although it may be difficult to get compassion out of some individuals, I believe that it is inside of each of us.

Helping out the person near you who needs help is not only the neighborly thing to do but the right thing. Helping those in need is always the right decision.

If you give to those around you, good things will come back to you. Sometimes you won't be able to map events directly to previous ones, but every so often it'll happen. And when it does, it is an awesome feeling!

Be Involved in the Community

The great thing about any town, city, or community is that there are numerous organizations, clubs, and groups that you can get involved in. It doesn't matter if they are civic groups, religious based, or more social. Each of them allows you to be part of something bigger. Plus, this allows you to expand your compassion beyond just your neighborhood and toward an even greater good.

Now, think about community as something that doesn't have borders, and you start to see the real power. We are all part of something bigger than ourselves, and it feels good. Everyone is rewarded from the collective knowledge that takes the stage, and the people you meet in the audience and hallways turn into lifelong friends.

You can take a simple idea and turn it into something more by involving the community.

Remember that you can't only be giving. It is okay to ask for something in return as well.

As you move forward, walking down the path of amazing things, always keep in mind that although the world is huge, you can make it much smaller by having a small-town mentality.

CHAPTER

25

Workshifting

In 2009, Citrix, the creator of online productivity products GoToMeeting, GoToWebinar, and others, coined the term *workshifting*.

Workshifting means working anywhere in the world, at any time, using the technology at your fingertips. You are never constrained by cubicle walls or a formal office.

Citrix started a blog called Workshifting.com that gives practical advice, reviews products, and discusses all information surrounding how to successfully live and work in this manner. I'm now a contributor and always look forward to new posts when they are published.

This term started out as nothing more than a marketing initiative by Citrix, but has grown into a business movement. It is now about a lifestyle and an approach to business. Smart employees want to work this way, and savvy entrepreneurs realize it is a better way to get their company not only going but thriving.

Not all jobs can be done in this way. It is rather hard to cook a perfect sausage pizza, walk your client's dog, or build a house from anywhere other than right where you need to be. But, even a few years ago, could you have imagined a doctor performing surgery, a ballet instructor teaching a class, or pilots conducting air strikes from remote locations? All of those are now a reality, and as the technology gets more powerful, so will the variety of jobs that can be done remotely.

This is the ultimate balance between life and work, and if your job cannot be done remotely, perhaps there are tasks that can. If you ever stay late or go into work early to take care of certain tasks, perhaps instead you can do them remotely. It can't hurt to talk to your boss about the possibility, can it?

Although some people worry that work-shifting will isolate us from other people, it in fact brings us closer together.

You can be empowered through the technology at your fingertips to voice, video, or text message with clients and colleagues around the globe from anywhere you might be. Meetings can be held with some members in the company conference room while other attendees are remotely connected via their laptops or mobile devices.

Technology cannot be ignored when it comes to living a more successful and happy life. It empowers you to work more efficiently, and every day there are new devices and services being created that can further help you. If technology is something that you rarely use, it is time to embrace it to determine where it can help you directly. If you need ideas on where to get started, Workshifting.com is a great place to begin reading.

Workshifting should also be viewed as giving you the freedom to work on your terms. It is much more about a mind-set and lifestyle than a suite of technologies that empower you to live that way.

Punching the 9-to-5 time clock hasn't been squashed yet, but when do you get most of your work done? Are you more efficient first thing in the morning or late at night? This allows you to be more flexible with your daytime hours.

Take out your notebook, open to a new page, and write down the header of "Work Tasks"; next, make a list of all the daily tasks that must be done from your office. Then list all the tasks that you do that could be accomplished from anywhere. Tasks such as invoicing, writing up performance reviews, and anything that involves looking at a computer screen can usually be done elsewhere.

Start by taking one day this week and do those tasks in a totally new location. This may mean going to a conference room or a local café at lunch to start. Yes, it'll feel weird at first, but after you've done it once, you'll realize that, like everyone, you have tasks that don't require you to sit at your desk to accomplish them.

Determining tasks that can be done outside of the office is one thing, but convincing your manager(s) that this is a good idea is a whole other ball of wax.

Be honest and direct with them when you ask about the possibility of working home for a few hours this week so that you can concentrate on getting these tasks done. Highlight that you won't have the distractions that come with every office environment and that you'd be very productive.

The key is that you must show that you are, in fact, productive. Although you won't be in the office, you'll still have distractions, so you must be disciplined to be successful.

Once you've demonstrated that you can get the work done even if they can't see you, it'll be easier to do it again in the future.

Thousands of people work like this every day around the world, so it will continue to get easier and more accepted. But to be given the chance to do it more often, you must first prove that you can work this way.

No matter if you are in an office or work-shifting from a café, you must get the needed work done to live and work this way. You may stumble, become frustrated, or run into obstacles along the way. As with anything, the more you do it, the more natural it will become. The better you do it, the more accepting your peers and superiors will become.

Workshifting empowers you and opens up new doors of opportunity for you and your career. Embracing this approach to work makes anything possible.

CHAPTER

26

Rules Are Like Rubber Bands

One question that comes up often when I am speaking to a group is, how did I know it was the right time to _____? The blank is sometimes filled in with start blogging, other times it is in reference to founding my own marketing agency, and once in a while it is about writing a book.

My answer is always the same, "Because no one told me I couldn't."

In every situation in life, there will be rules or standards that are in place. Ask why they are there, and sometimes the answer is because it is the way it has always been done. Those are the rules that really restrict creative thinking or expression, because many of them never get revisited or changed. And why would they? No one has ever questioned them.

If you want to be happier, you must bend the rules as much as possible in your favor.

Think about any rules that bother you. Now, think about all the ways that you can bend these rules without ever breaking them.

With rules, you have to realize that you can bend them only so far before something (or someone) will snap, and you'll suffer a bit of pain from it. This is why thinking about them as rubber bands is crucial. We've all been stung by one that snapped when stretched too far.

Any teenager can tell you about a time he or she went too far when challenging his or her parents. We've all done it. Rebelling is accepted as part of being a teenager. But why do we outgrow this and decide to conform as we get older?

The only way you can find the limits of a particular policy or norm is by pushing until you discover where the limit is. Sure, some snaps are more painful than others, and depending on what you are bending, sometimes you have to be more careful than others.

If you're in a work situation where you are dealing with a manager or anyone higher on the org chart than yourself, you've got to be extra smart about what you are doing. Questioning a policy or rule is one thing. But to openly and blatantly defy something could end in being demoted or even fired. Always be smart with your rule bending.

I'm not advocating for open insubordination. Rather, you should never live life as just another drone or sheep doing whatever you are told. Anyone who wants to be a cubicle slave the rest of his or her life probably wouldn't be reading this book anyway.

Never be afraid of fighting for what you believe in and anything you think can help you achieve your dreams. If everyone colors inside of the lines all the time, the world is going to get boring in a rapid fashion.

Stretch, push, and strive to make the world what you need it to be. Some rules are put in place to protect you, but too many feel like all they are doing is stifling you and your success. Don't let that happen.

27

Beer and Coffee

Independent musician and piano rocker Matthew Ebel has a great album titled *Beer and Coffee*. I'm hoping he doesn't mind me borrowing it, because I feel this combination is a cornerstone of living your life to the fullest.

We live in a world where if we didn't want to, we'd never have to leave the house to have real-world, face-to-face contact with others. Our devices empower us to connect with people around the globe at any hour of the day. Although it is great to have that ability, seeing people face-to-face offers levels of interaction and connection not possible through technology.

Plenty of amazing opportunities can and will come about through your online networks. But when you want more than that, going out and meeting people is even better. To have amazing things happen to you, you need to step away from your screens and make sure you stay engaged with people. You've got to live beyond a social network to get the most out of life. Handshakes and hugs will always trump likes and shares.

Right now, in cities around the world and small towns down the road, people are sitting down over a drink of some sort and having a conversation. Some are talking about business and trying to sign a deal. Others just finished attending church and are catching up on the latest gossip. Some are meeting for the first time, and a relationship is being formed.

If it is hard for you to make it to events where colleagues or peers gather, schedule one-on-one catch-ups with friends and colleagues as often as possible.

You don't need an agenda or preconceived plans. It is more about spending time together. But guess what happens? More often than not, something along the lines of, "Have you heard about . . . ?" or "Do you know . . . ?" is asked, and that leads to something new and exciting.

Plus, sitting down with a friend allows you to hug, shake hands, and look into your friend's eyes while talking. Being in the same space allows you to really connect with each other, rather than looking at a screen and being distracted by a million different things.

Beer and coffee is also a bigger metaphor for the type of gatherings you should be keeping.

The coffee represents the smaller gatherings— one-on-ones or more intimate conversations that make up for the lack of quantity of people in the quality of the conversation.

The beer gatherings are typically larger— more people whom you are connecting with and catching up with, but they don't allow for the deep level of conversation that you can have in a smaller gathering.

Of course, larger social gatherings may include people you don't know. Making it a point to introduce yourself to the people you don't know is always a great idea. If you are in a room full of people, there is never a reason to be standing alone. This is your time to connect, say hello, and let people know who you are.

Just don't start by throwing around your credentials or name-dropping the minute you meet people. You never want to be that person; no one likes that sort of person. Say hi, listen, let other people talk more, and really pay attention to what they are saying. It shows that you care about what they are saying, and you'll remember much more about them that way.

Socializing is something many people are forgetting how to do because of the growth of the Web. Social media surrounds us, yet everyone seems to skip over the social part.

Get out. Meet people. Put away your devices. Grab a drink. Share a meal. Enjoy every minute of it!

28

Hallway Magic

Every March I get excited as I board a plane for Austin, Texas, to attend the annual South by Southwest (SXSW) Conference. Over the years, this has grown from a fairly small crowd of tech, music, and film fans into a pilgrimage of tens of thousands of people from every walk of life converging in Austin.

Although it has gotten larger and perhaps more difficult to connect with people, the serendipity of it is the hallway magic.

This doesn't just happen at SXSW, but I notice it here more than any other conference I attend. You never know when you might suddenly cross paths with or bump into someone who will become a friend, business partner, or just a great person to talk to.

With 25,000-plus people walking around, the chances of crossing paths with an old friend are in your favor and completely against you at the same time.

Of course, this can and does happen at any kind of event or gathering. You have just as much chance of hallway magic happening the next time you sit down on an airplane or wait in line at your local coffee shop.

When you go looking for it, you'll rarely find it. One cannot plan for serendipity, but by getting out there and talking to strangers, you can be sure it'll happen to you.

Hallway magic can't happen if you never leave the house, so make sure you find the time to get out. Call that friend you haven't seen in a long time, buy tickets to a sporting event, or go to the mall for a few hours. Whatever you do, the more people around you, the better the chance of something magical happening.

Don't forget that the Earth is a big place, but you can make it feel smaller by experiencing as much of the world as possible.

You need to be open to new experiences to increase your chances of hallway magic happening. Get on a train, board an airplane, or jump into the car. It doesn't matter if you visit a far off corner of the globe or Main Street in the next town over. You can always find and experience something new wherever your feet land.

Whatever you do and wherever your life takes you, let your heart and mind always remain open. Serendipity doesn't appreciate a closed soul and hallway magic is reserved for those willing to accept it.

29

Celebrate Success of All Sizes

How many times have you been reprimanded, corrected, or scolded for minor actions? Now, think about how many times you've been patted on the back, congratulated, or rewarded for other small actions. I'm willing to bet that you can think of more of the first than the second.

We're all guilty of being quick to correct situations while not recognizing or rewarding behaviors where great things are accomplished. If you want to be happier, you've got to learn to celebrate all levels of success.

We are taught to celebrate major milestones. New jobs, babies, and awards are always a good place to start. But what about the smaller victories that might happen daily? Why are we not celebrating those?

Life is much happier when we are celebrating. It is hard to argue with that. Thus, more celebrating equals a happier life.

Take the time to recognize even the simplest of victories. There will be plenty of struggles, and having memories of your successes and celebrations are good to look back on—a bit of light when stuck in a cave of darkness.

Be sure to also celebrate those around you. Those types of things are remembered, appreciated, and most often are returned to you in the future.

Take out your notebook and write "Way to Go!" at the top of a new page. Under that, write down everything you've done in the past three weeks that made you feel good. Perhaps you got up early and hit the gym, successfully cooked a new recipe, or managed to push through a task that had been hanging over your head for too long. If it made you smile, write it down.

As you look at the list, ask yourself if you celebrated any of them. If not, what can you do to celebrate similar victories in the future?

Remember that celebrating doesn't mean you have to throw a party or get a trophy. You should think of celebrations as an excuse to do anything that gives you pleasure. Something as small as 15 minutes of pleasure reading, playing a video game, or drinking a glass of wine can be a satisfying celebration.

The next time you are working on a task that you are having a hard time finishing, tell yourself that if you complete it, you get to celebrate. These little mental games always help me, and I bet they'll help you.

Of course, when you achieve something greater, there is nothing wrong with going a bit crazy with the celebration. I have a tradition of purchasing myself an expensive bottle of scotch or tequila for big life-changing milestones. When I finished my first book, my wife surprised me with a bottle of Macallan 25 scotch that I had always wanted to try. This made all the hard work worth it.

Life is a series of experiences, and by making more of them uplifting and celebratory, you'll balance out the bad and frustrating.

Let me be the first to celebrate you taking the first steps toward the life you've been dreaming about!

CHAPTER

30

Learn from Failure, But Don't Seek It Out

There is a recent fascination with failure and encouraging people to embrace it. Do a quick search, and in books, articles, and blog posts, you'll find the "fail fast; fail often" cadre.

Failure is going to happen in your life. No one is successful all the time, but this notion that anyone should be encouraged to fail is a dangerous way to proceed.

Failure is a part of life. You will crash and burn. That great idea you have really isn't as good as you think, and no one will like it. You will make many mistakes along the way. But people are not judged by their failures, but rather how they pick themselves up after the fact.

Do not embrace or look for failure. Accept that it will happen, and when it does learn from it.

When you do fail, try to do it as quickly as possible.

Knowing if or when to quit is extremely important if you are failing at something. The last thing you ever want to do is have failure stretch out. That taps time, money, and sanity that you could be using toward new and exciting things.

Even with failure a guaranteed part of life, this does not mean that you should ever welcome it. You need to always strive for success and work as hard as possible toward your dreams at all times.

We've spent a lot of time together in these pages making sure that you are focusing on the most important things in your life. We've removed the fluff so that you know what really matters. Because you've done this and are now focused on the path you want to be on, it is more critical than ever to succeed.

Failure is mentioned because when it happens, you must continue on. Nothing is going to be handed to you, and hard work tinged with struggle comes with the territory. Being aware of your enemies (in this case failure) and doing everything in your power to avoid them is what you need to take away from this.

CHAPTER

31

Don't Let the Asshats and Ankle Biters Get You Down

Realize right now that not everyone is going to embrace the path you choose to follow. You will have doubters, skeptics, and haters no matter what you do. If you don't have them, then you are not stretching yourself enough.

UrbanDicationary.com defines a *troll* as: "One who posts a deliberately provocative message to a newsgroup or message board with the intention of causing maximum disruption and argument."

This may be an online-focused definition, but there are just as many trolls in the real world as well. Similar to those you find on the Internet, they walk among us just looking to cause trouble, without any clear focus on who they bother, as long as they bother someone.

The simple rule is to never feed the trolls.

They thrive off of attention, and any that you give them will encourage them to not only hang around but also throw more insults at you. It is never easy, but you should ignore them and move on.

Although trolls fling hate aimlessly, they long to stir the pot without ever adding anything to it. They tend to be easy to identify and move past once you know what to look for.

But, trolls aren't the type of people who are going to hold you back from being happy or successful. Those types of people I've dubbed asshats and ankle biters.

An *asshat* is someone who is clearly misguided. Asshats believe that what they are doing is correct and proper, but in reality, they are clueless about the actions they are taking. You often will find them inside of a company in a position of power. They are easy to spot as the ones who will pay for an expert consultant to come in and then not follow any of the guidance that the expert gave.

Asshats are related to, but different from, douchebags, jackwads, and idiots. Distant cousins include the snake oil salesmen, infomercial hosts, and television preachers. In today's online world, many of them have adopted a title that might involve words like rock star, guru, or Jedi.

What makes asshats so difficult to deal with is that they are not actually clueless—at least not completely. In most cases they are actually intelligent people who have lost their way. They've obtained a certain level of notoriety or power, and it goes to their heads. They make irrational decisions and inaccurate statements that you didn't ask for.

Ankle biters are similar in their annoying nature, but they usually don't have the power or the level of influence of asshats—but they crave it more than anything else.

They can be easy to spot because they are usually openly challenging your ideas or opinions. No matter what you say, they have a counterpoint. They can't accept the thoughts of others and must constantly have their say. Many will try to be clever or witty and try to leverage humor on their side to mask their intentions.

These people will always butt in on conversations they have no part of to try to seem relevant. Never reply to ankle biters, no matter what they say. They thrive off of your reactions.

The thing that you must remember with all of these types is that they have power only if you pay attention to them. With trolls and ankle biters, you can ignore them most of the time and move on. The problem comes with asshats, because they usually have at least some ability to affect you. It is common for them to be close to you in either your business or professional life.

Entire books are written on how to deal with these types of people because they come in so many different forms. You'll never be able to escape them in your life, but you can figure out how to minimize the amount of contact you need to have with them and how much control or influence they have on your life.

The key is to recognize them as quickly as possible. That way you can avoid them and not be concerned with their doubts, hate, or rantings.

Be sure that you balance out your life by surrounding yourself with good souls who will fill you with encouragement, inspiration, and positive notions. None of us live in Eden, but we can do all that is in our power to not let what we don't like to get to us.

And never forget what you learned to say earlier: "To each their own!"

32

Can You Idle Well?

Life is fast paced. We all wish we could have more hours in a day to get everything done that we'd like to. Because of that, we are in a constant state of motion, moving from one thing to the next.

To be truly happy and fully enjoy life, you need to slow down—not just once in a while, but regularly.

I'm also not talking about only slowing down for an hour or less. I'm talking about completely shutting down and taking in the world around you by doing nothing.

I learned a key phrase during a weeklong excursion into the backcountry of the Boundary Waters Wilderness with my father. For a week it was just us, our canoe, and the wilderness.

One afternoon, as we sat there looking out into the vast beauty surrounding us after several days of not seeing another human being, my dad broke the silence with, "We sure do know how to idle well."

As random as it was, it was perfect poetry for the situation. Ever since then, I've adopted this mantra. And I strive to do it every single day, even if only for a little bit.

When was the last time you took even 15 minutes to do absolutely nothing? No phone. No music. Nothing except you and your wandering thoughts.

Try it now. Wherever you are, put down the book, turn off all electronics, close a door if you can, and idle for 15 minutes. Don't worry. Everything and everyone will be there when you are done.

It probably felt a little weird and strange, but the longer you sat there and embraced being idle didn't it feel great? It gets easier the more you do it.

Now would be a good time to talk about being idle for longer than only a short break.

No matter what our job is, taking vacation time for a day, week, or more isn't easy because there is always more work to be done. If you are a business owner or self-employed, than any time not working could mean missing out on potential income. But, remember what we said about making excuses earlier?

Leaving the office behind and unplugging from work is critical to living a more fulfilling life. The purpose of taking a vacation or a personal day is to recharge your batteries and enjoy the time away. If you spend all that time checking your voice mail or replying to e-mails than why did you take the time off in the first place?

Idle time is productive time if you let it be.

Most people will find that when they let their minds go, it tends to focus on things they've been thinking about. Perhaps for you, this would work when you are in bed before going to sleep, on an airplane, or on your lunch break. Once you start slowing your mind down and allowing it to roam, your mind tends to come up with new ideas, solutions to problems you are facing, and other amazing things.

Although you can't always schedule "idle time," you need to embrace the concept so that you allow yourself to do it. The longer you can idle, the more relaxed your brain will become— and that is when the magic happens.

CHAPTER
33

Giving Back and Gratitude

Although this chapter may come toward the end of the book, I believe that it is one of the most important aspects of living the successful and happy life that you are striving for.

It is critical that each of us remember that none of us can be successful without the help of others. This is why we surround ourselves with great friends and good people.

Never forget two of the most important words you can ever say: thank you.

No act of kindness is too small for you to show your gratitude, and it is impossible to say thank you too much.

Want to take it a step further? For those who go above and beyond the basic acts of kindness, consider sending a handwritten thank-you card. Although this is old-fashioned and takes longer than sending an e-mail or a text message, I promise you that the person will appreciate it, and doing so shows how much you appreciate that person's help.

Also it is important that you give back to the world around you. Find charities and organizations that you believe in and find a way to help them. The easy answer is to give them money, but what is more rewarding (and many times more helpful) is donating your time and experience.

Each of us is unique in the ways we can help out others, and you need to make sure that you are always giving back. It helps round you out as a good person, and at the same time, nothing feels better than helping out those in need.

I've been blessed to work with a variety of different organizations over the years. Most recently, I've started working with the ONE campaign, helping advocate for the end of poverty and hunger in the world. I also serve on the board of directors for Wediko, which helps emotionally distraught kids live a fulfilling life.

On top of those, I try to donate a few dollars every time I see a friend raising money for a good cause, and every year, I try to make some form of donation to my favorite charity, Fisher House, who builds houses near military hospitals for families of wounded soldiers to live in during treatment.

No matter what line of work you are in, make sure to find a way to volunteer and give back to at least one cause you believe in.

The world is a massive place, but thanks to technology, it can feel smaller every day. There is a never-ending stream of worthy causes that you can help. Take some time to search on Charity

Navigator to find the organizations that operate in a way you agree with and that are working toward the causes you are passionate about.

A core part of living a happy and successful life is being helpful to others. Never, ever forget that.

Thank you.

CHAPTER

34

Play in the Rain

When was the last time you went out and played in the rain?

Most of us did this as children, but have you done it recently? When was the last time you saw a downpour on a hot summer day and decided to run out and feel the instant cool? Or jumped into that massive puddle that formed on the side of the road to see how high you could splash it?

Here is the great thing about playing in the rain and why it is one of the final thoughts I want to leave you with as we approach the end of the book.

It is the perfect metaphor for walking on the path you are now taking. Things get messy. Sometimes it is dangerous, and it isn't what most consider normal. Yet, it is also exhilarating, inspiring, and fun!

A lot of situations are just like this. It looks dark and scary, and most people would rather avoid getting involved. But I'm encouraging you to dive right in.

The road less traveled isn't a smooth one, but it sure is awesome!

Life is too short to be shackled by constraints that other people put in place. Of course, your first instinct if your kids asked if they could go play in the rain would be to say no. The same thing goes for others around you. But we are of a different ilk, and we know that the rewards far outweigh the risks.

Jump in the puddle. Throw your arms out, and look to the sky in glee. Doesn't it feel amazing?

35

The End and the Beginning

This is the end of the book, but it's the start of something amazing for you.

My goal is to give you enough motivation to push you forward with whatever dream you've only been thinking about until now. If you didn't yell out at least once either in celebration or damnation toward me, then I've failed.

Sure, not everyone is going to enjoy or appreciate what I've written, but I'd be lying if I said I didn't hope that those individuals are few and far between. I want this book to resonate with people. My hope is that many of you will be motivated enough to make the changes in your life to do what you really want to accomplish.

I started the book by promising you nothing but honesty and advice that has helped me. I'm hoping that at least one nugget (and hopefully more) has resonated with you and that at some point in the future you'll be able to look back at reading this book as helping you on your way to success.

Of course, that is up to you and the hard work you must put in to make your life whatever it is you want it to be. I'm still working every day to get closer to my goals and dreams. I'm very happy with where my life is at right now, but there are still mountains to climb and finishing lines to cross.

This is the beginning of the next phase of your life, and I can't wait to hear what you do with it. Please keep me updated on your progress by visiting me at CC-Chapman.com.

I'm eager to hear about all the amazing things that have happened to you.

Peace and be wild!

Dangerous Books

I t is vital that you never stop consuming information in your life. Making the time to read on a regular basis is critical to a more satisfying life.

I refer to these books as "dangerous" because each of them sparked something in my mind that set me off in a new direction, and someone who is comfortable in his or her current life might not want to have that spark go off—hence the danger.

Hopefully, like me, you'll find them inspiring and helpful.

First, Break All the Rules, by Marcus Buckingham

This was the first book that gave me permission to not follow the rules.

The Dip, by Seth Godin

This book makes the list because while reading it, I determined that I had to set off on my own and break away from the agency I was working with. The focus is on how you have to know when to quit and move on and how too many people get stuck in the dip and never get out of it.

The Flinch, by Julien Smith

If you want to be challenged by a book to embrace your fears and not only push through them but stomp them under your foot, this is a must-read for you. It is a blunt and in-your-face manifesto to help anyone deal with risk aversion.

Made to Stick, by Chip and Dan Heath

This book has everything to do with the mind-set and approach that people need to take if they want to make an impression in today's socially connected and always on world.

Ignore Everybody, by Hugh MacLeod

Who would believe that a cartoonist could teach you so much about believing in yourself and following your heart?

The 48 Laws of Power, by Robert Greene

The laws are laid out one by one with accompanying examples and stories from throughout history to back each of them up. Sure, some of them are over the top and may go against your principles, but just like rules, you can bend these laws to fit your life and journey.

Rules of the Red Rubber Ball, by Kevin Carroll

There isn't much dangerous about this book, but it really should be on everyone's desk throughout the world because it is the perfect mix of inspiration and playful spirit that we need more of.

Oh, the Places You'll Go! by Dr. Seuss

How can you argue with the king of playful philosophy? Every time I read this, I find another reason to smile and am reminded of how to live a great life.